T0210125

THE
BIBLE'S
HIDDEN TREASURE

JAMES: THE PRECIOUS PEARL

JOHN P. HAGEMAN, M.S., C.H.P.

WESTBOW
P R E S S®
A DIVISION OF THOMAS NELSON
& ZONDERVAN

WestBow Press books may be ordered through booksellers or by contacting:

WestBow Press
A Division of Thomas Nelson & Zondervan
1663 Liberty Drive
Bloomington, IN 47403
www.westbowpress.com
1 (866) 928-1240

ISBN: 978-1-9736-9285-0 (sc)
ISBN: 978-1-9736-9286-7 (hc)
ISBN: 978-1-9736-9284-3 (e)

Library of Congress Control Number: 2020910136

Print information available on the last page.

WestBow Press rev. date: 6/27/2020

DEDICATION

The *Bible's Hidden Treasure* is dedicated to my wife and two daughters. It is also dedicated to all the Christian teachers who are doing their best to lead people to Christ and to the narrow path that God wants us to walk to achieve salvation.

ACKNOWLEDGMENT

I want to thank Ty Hall for his encouragement, constructive comments, and editorial suggestions.

PROLOGUE

If James were here today, he might say, "As a servant of God and of the Lord Jesus Christ, I wrote my letter to the twelve tribes of Israel, scattered among the nations, so that this message will be seen and read by the entire world. This letter goes to the heart of God's truth about our seeking salvation. Some may contradict what is in my letter, but I know that God's absolute truth can be found with heavenly inspired wisdom and that His truth will ultimately prevail."

CONTENTS

Introduction xv

Chapter 1   Are You Saved by Faith Alone? 1
Chapter 2   Does God Change with Time? 7
Chapter 3   Which of the Ten Commandments Is the
Least Important? 10
Chapter 4   What Is God-Given Wisdom, and How Do
You Get It? 20
Chapter 5   Does God Tempt You, and Where Does
Temptation Lead You? 26
Chapter 6   How Is Facing Trials Good for You? 31
Chapter 7   What about Patience and Perseverance? 34
Chapter 8   Are You Rich? Do You Show Favoritism? 40
Chapter 9   Do You Have an Alligator Mouth? 49
Chapter 10   What Works and Deeds Are Important? 54
Chapter 11   Do You Judge Others? 60
Chapter 12   Are You a Friend of the World? 64
Chapter 13   Will You Act Today, or Only Listen to What
You Must Do? 66
Chapter 14   What Else Should You Pray For? 69
Chapter 15   Why Is the Book of James the Precious Pearl? 71
Chapter 16   Are There Contradictory Passages in the Bible? 73
Chapter 17   Why I Wrote This Book 91

About the Author 95

INTRODUCTION

This book's primary goal is to lead us on our most important quest: to discover, understand, and travel on our path to heaven. Our narrow path to heaven is simply obedience to God's will and His commandments. One person told me the whole concept of the Bible might be summed up in four words: do good, resist evil. The tough question is, how do we do this? The Bible is an excellent guidebook, with all the dos and don'ts that tell us how to lead our lives in order to stay on our narrow path to salvation and heaven.

It is vital to get to the heart of God's absolute truth in the Bible, so that we can reorganize and prioritize our lives to start walking on the straight and narrow path of righteousness as soon as possible. Considering there is so little time in our lives to do this, compared to eternity, we should start as soon as possible. I found one book of the Bible, the short book of James, to be like a hidden treasure or a precious pearl, as discussed in the parable told by Jesus in Matthew 13:44–46:

> The kingdom of heaven is like treasure hidden in a field. When a man found it, he hid it again, and then in his joy went and sold all he had and bought that field. Again, the kingdom of heaven is like a merchant looking for fine pearls. When he found one of great value, he went away and sold everything he had and bought it. (NIV)

The book of James is this precious pearl; and you should give up everything else to possess this treasure that will lead you to your salvation. Chapter 1 starts with the key question, are you saved by faith alone? The book of James answers this question with a definite no. The following chapters address many concerns and topics brought out in James's book that clearly lead you to the straight and narrow path that God wants you to walk on, to gain eternal life and a place in heaven. Other chapters include the following:

- Does God Change with Time?
- Which of the Ten Commandments Is the Least Important?
- What Is God-Given Wisdom, and How Do You Get It?
- Does God Tempt You?
- How Is Facing Trials Good for You?
- What about Patience and Perseverance?
- Are You Rich? Do You Show Favoritism?
- Do You Have an Alligator Mouth?
- What Works and Deeds Are Important?
- Do You Judge Others?
- Are You a Friend of the World?
- Will You Act Today or Only Listen to What You Must Do?
- What Else Should You Pray For?

Do you ask yourself some of these questions? Do you want concrete answers to these questions? The small book of James truly has the answers you are seeking. I pray that you find heavenly wisdom in this book and that you will share it with as many others as possible.

Objective analysis of the Bible concludes that God's truth is in there, despite some human-made contradictions. I say human-made contradictions because every word in the Bible is written by humans, who are not perfect. Would God, who is perfect, allow contradictory material to be inserted in the Bible? Since God gave us all a free will, it is possible that some contradictions could be inserted into the Bible. Some of the contradictions in the Bible are discussed in this book.

CHAPTER 1

ARE YOU SAVED BY FAITH ALONE?

One of the central beliefs in the Protestant doctrine is that you are saved by faith alone. This is the fundamental teaching of the founder of the Protestant movement, Martin Luther. What does the Bible specifically say about whether you are saved by faith alone? In the entire Bible, the phrase "faith alone" only appears once.

What good is it, my brothers and sisters, if someone claims to have faith but has no deeds? Can such faith save them? Suppose a brother or a sister is without clothes and daily food. If one of you says to them, "Go in peace; keep warm and well fed," but does nothing about their physical needs, what good is it? In the same way, faith by itself, if it is not accompanied by action, is dead. But someone will say, "You have faith; I have deeds." Show me your faith without deeds, and I will show you my faith by my deeds. **You believe that there is one God. Good! Even the demons believe that—and shudder.** You foolish person, do you want evidence that faith without deeds is useless? Was not our father Abraham considered righteous for what he did when he offered his son Isaac on the altar? You see that his faith and his actions were working together, and his faith was made complete by what he did. And the scripture was fulfilled that says, "Abraham believed God, and it was credited to him as righteousness," and he was called God's friend. **You see that a person is considered righteous by what they do and not by faith alone.** In the same way, was not even Rahab the prostitute considered righteous for what she did when she gave lodging to the spies and sent them off in a different direction? **As the body without the spirit is dead, so faith without deeds is dead**. (James 2:14–26 NIV; bold added)

There are at least four good examples of biblical texts that both support and refute Martin Luther's proclamation that you are saved (justified) by faith alone. The following examples show the differences of whether or not you are saved by faith alone.

Example 1

Saved by faith alone:

For it is by grace you have been saved, through faith—and this is not from yourselves, it is the gift of God—-not by works, so that no one can boast. (Ephesians 2:8–9 NIV)

Saved by works:

For of this you can be sure: No immoral, impure or greedy person—such a person is an idolater—has any inheritance in the kingdom of Christ and of God. (Ephesians 5:5 NIV)

(Which of us, who has total faith in Jesus, has acted in an immoral, impure, or greedy manner? If so, then even with that faith, aren't our impure actions still condemning us to hell?)

Example 2

Saved by faith alone:

> We who are Jews by birth and not sinful Gentiles know that a person is not justified by the works of the law, but by faith in Jesus Christ. So we, too, have put our faith in Christ Jesus that **we may be justified by faith** in Christ and not by the works of the law, **because by the works of the law no one will be justified.** (Galatians 2:15–16 NIV; bold added)

Saved by works:

> Do not be deceived: God cannot be mocked. **A man reaps what he sows.** Whoever sows to please their flesh, from the flesh will reap destruction; **whoever sows to please the Spirit, from the Spirit will reap eternal life. Let us not become weary in doing good, for at the proper time we will reap a harvest if we do not give up.** Therefore, as we have opportunity, let us do good to all people, especially to those who belong to the family of believers. (Galatians 6:7–10 NIV; bold added)

Example 3

Saved by faith alone:

> For we maintain that **a person is justified by faith** apart from the works of the law. (Romans 3:28 NIV; bold added)

Saved by works:

> God "**will repay each person according to what they have done.**" To those who by **persistence in doing good seek glory, honor and immortality, He will give eternal life.** (Romans 2:6–7 NIV; bold added)

Is Paul delivering contradictory messages within each of his letters that he sent to Christ's disciples? Is he speaking out of both sides of his mouth? Which of his words do you want to believe and have faith in? By the way, *belief* and *faith* mean the same thing.

Example 4

Saved by faith alone:

> What is more, I consider everything a loss because of the surpassing worth of knowing Christ Jesus my Lord, for whose sake I have lost all things. I consider them garbage, that I may gain Christ and be found in him, **not having a righteousness of my own that comes from the law, but that which is through faith in Christ—the righteousness that comes from God on the basis of faith.** (Philippians 3:8–9 NIV; bold added)

Saved by works:

> But just as He who called you is holy, **so be holy in all you do**; for it is written: "Be holy, because I am holy." Since you call on a **Father Who judges each person's work impartially**, live out your time as foreigners here in reverent fear. (1 Peter 1:15–17 NIV; bold added)

All of these saved-by-faith-alone texts come from Paul, formerly

Saul, who proclaimed himself to be an apostle of Jesus Christ. Is Paul to be believed over James? In any search to find the truth, you must ask a lot of questions. For example, when detectives question suspects, they look for inconsistencies in their stories by asking the suspects to repeat their stories or alibies several times. Inconsistencies in their stories raise questions about their honesty. There certainly are contradictions within the first three examples, which were written by Paul. Later, in an analysis of Saul's three versions of his story of his trip to Damascus, can questions about inconsistencies be raised? Chapter 16 discusses this.

Ask yourself which of these contradictory statements about being saved is the truth. Are we saved by faith alone or by our works? How easy would it be if just believing that Jesus Christ is the Son of God gave you a free pass into heaven? If that's true, the devil who tempted Jesus in the desert believes this, so does he get to go to heaven? Does such faith without making changes in your lifestyle guarantee your salvation? On the other hand, can your works and deeds make you more worthy of God's grace? We are all sinners, and we need a whole lot of God's grace to be forgiven for all the sins of our past. If it does take your works and deeds to lead to your salvation—as my mother used to say—you've got a tough row to hoe.

Are you saved simply because you believe or have faith? Wouldn't it be great if simply believing in something would make it true? I have learned that if something sounds too good to be true, it probably is too good to be true. Don't you consider that the value of what you own is equal to what you paid for it or how hard you had to work to get it? If everyone were to get a college diploma simply because they believe they deserve one, what would those diplomas be worth? Absolutely nothing. And how many stories are there where a person wins the lottery to only squander all of their cheaply won fortune within a short period of time? Aren't things that are cheap worth exactly that?

Many Christians believe that only those who believe that Jesus Christ is God will go to heaven. Is this true? If so, all other religious people, like Jews, Hindus, Buddhist, Sikhs, and Muslims, cannot or will not go to heaven. I asked this question myself and found the answer in the Bible. If there is even one person who got into heaven who was not a believer that Christ is God, then the idea that only Christians will go to heaven is a false premise. 2 Kings 2:1–18 tells of the Lord taking Elijah up into heaven, which happened long before anyone knew anything about Jesus Christ. If there is one exception to a rule, then that rule is no longer valid.

Could it be that people, like Elijah, can go to heaven based on their works and deeds on earth and not simply believing that Jesus Christ is God? Also, who are we to decide who is saved or fit to go to heaven? Isn't that a decision that only God can make?

CHAPTER 2

DOES GOD CHANGE WITH TIME?

God must be perfect and unwavering in His rule if He is to be fully trusted. If God changes His positions and laws with time, His credibility can be questioned. Does the Bible present information that indicates God changed His rules for humans over time? Again, remember that humans, all of whom have faults, held the pens that wrote the Bible. Might it be possible that they wrote some verses in the Bible that were not exactly what God wanted them to write? In James 1:16–18, the question of whether God changes with time is clearly answered.

> Don't be deceived, my dear brothers and sisters. Every good and perfect gift is from above, coming down from **the Father of the heavenly lights, Who does not change like shifting shadows**. He chose to give us birth through the word of truth, that we might be a kind of first fruits of all He created. (James 1:16–18 NIV, bold added)

Do you wonder why God required His chosen people, the Israelites, to make animal blood sacrifices to please Him? Why doesn't God still require animal sacrifices today? Did God change His mind about animal sacrifices? The theological consensus is that Jesus Christ's sacrifice on the cross is the replacement for animal sacrifices; thus, we don't need that bloody practice anymore. I'm not too sure about that consensus. How can we trust a God Who requires one thing one day and something else the next? Changing or shifting a major position, rule, or law is inconsistent and does not meet the standard of a perfect God. It would be more like the action of politicians who change their minds based on public opinion or well-funded lobbyists.

I think a hint of the uselessness of blood sacrifices is given in the story of Abraham. God tested Abraham, asking him to sacrifice his own son, Isaac, and then at the last minute spared Isaac, indicating that a blood sacrifice was unnecessary. (See the full story at Genesis 22:1–19.) Also, see what is said about burnt offerings and sacrifices in Mark 12:33. (Mark 12:28–34 is quoted in chapter 3.) Here is another example of God not wanting animal sacrifices and burnt offerings:

> Solomon made an alliance with Pharaoh king of Egypt and married his daughter. He brought her to the City of David until he finished building his palace and the temple of the LORD, and the wall around Jerusalem. The people, however, were still sacrificing at the high places, because a temple had not yet been built for the Name of the LORD. Solomon showed his love for the LORD by walking according to the instructions given him by his father David, except that he offered sacrifices and burned incense on the high places. (1 Kings 3:1–3 NIV)

The Old Testament supports this idea that God does not change with time:

God is not human, that He should lie, **not a human being, that He should change His mind**. Does He speak and then not act? Does He promise and not fulfill? (Numbers 23:19 NIV, bold added)

God, Who is enthroned from of old, Who does not change—He will hear them and humble them, because they have no fear of God. My companion attacks his friends; he violates his covenant. His talk is smooth as butter, yet war is in his heart; his words are more soothing than oil, yet they are drawn swords. Cast your cares on the LORD and He will sustain you; He will never let the righteous be shaken. (Psalm 55:19–22 NIV, bold added)

To trust and believe in a perfect God requires that the Lord must not change over time.

God's perfect and absolute truth in the New Testament must be exactly the same as that in the Old Testament. If not, are you listening to words that sound as smooth as butter; while hiding the swords that will cut you off from the Lord's absolute truth?

CHAPTER 3

WHICH OF THE TEN COMMANDMENTS IS THE LEAST IMPORTANT?

The importance of God and His true words being unchanging and chiseled in stone can be further examined by looking at the Ten Commandments. Do all of the Lord's Ten Commandments still apply today? Do each of His commandments have equal weight and value, or can one commandment be less of a sin if broken? Here is what James says about the Ten Commandments, in James 2:10–11.

> For whoever keeps the whole law and yet **stumbles at just one point is guilty of breaking all of it.** For He who said, "You shall not commit adultery," also said, "You shall not murder." If you do not commit adultery but do commit murder, you have become a lawbreaker. (James 2:10–11 NIV, bold added)

You may consider murder to be much worse than adultery. But is that really correct? Is that what God thinks? Or is that a judgment made by humans on their feelings about the relative severity of these two different sins? If you simply switch the wording order, in James 2:11, and exchange murder with adultery, the context of the sentence still carries the same intent. If you do not murder but do commit adultery, you have become a lawbreaker, guilty of breaking the full set of commandments. Are these two commandments equally important? If you never murder anyone, but you steal, lie against your neighbor, or commit adultery, aren't you still guilty of breaking God's laws? If you break any one of God's laws (His Ten Commandments) that makes you a sinner, just the same as if you committed murder. People think that premeditated murder is the most evil crime. But ask yourself, what act of adultery is not premeditated, and isn't that just as serious an infraction of God's commandments?

An important point: trying to decide if any commandment is more or less important means you are trying to judge or weigh God's laws:

> Brothers and sisters, do not slander one another. Anyone who speaks against a brother or sister or judges them speaks against the law and judges it. **When you judge the law, you are not keeping it, but sitting in judgment on it. There is only one Lawgiver and Judge, the one Who is able to save and destroy.** But you—who are you to judge your neighbor? (James 4:11–12 NIV, bold added)

By judging which commandment(s) may or may not be important, aren't you acting like you have perfect knowledge and the wisdom of God Himself? Well, just who do you think you are? However, some Christians may consider one of the Ten Commandants unimportant or even irrelevant. Some commandments are short and clear; for example, don't murder, don't steal, and don't bear false witness. However, consider the longest of the ten, the fourth commandment. The fourth commandment is the longest (the most words) and is written that way to help make the full meaning very clear.

> Remember the Sabbath day by keeping it holy. Six days you shall labor and do all your work, but the seventh day is a sabbath to the LORD your God. On it you shall not do any work, neither you, nor your son or daughter, nor your male or female servant, nor your animals, nor any foreigner residing in your towns. For in six days the LORD made the heavens and the earth, the sea, and all that is in them, but he rested on the seventh day. Therefore the LORD blessed the Sabbath day and made it holy. (Exodus 20:8–11 NIV)

I would guess most people only focus on the first eight words of the fourth commandment and ignore the other ninety-one words. By merely keeping the Sabbath holy, many Christians can go to church on Sunday and then go out to brunch or lunch afterwards, to a restaurant to be served by waiters and cooks, who are paid workers and laborers. Is that really okay?

This commandment talks about labor and work, and people work or labor for wages. The fourth commandment goes further than just keeping the Sabbath holy, by telling you not to pay anyone to work for you on the Sabbath. This ban on paying others to work for you applies to your children, your servants, any foreigner residing in your towns, and even to working your animals for a profit. The part about foreigners applies to those nonbelievers, those not following God's commandments, who are willing to work on the Sabbath. Years ago, before the two-day weekend, it was a practice to have Jews work on Sunday for Christian companies, since the Jewish Sabbath is on Saturday. Wouldn't such practices by a Christian company violate the detailed and full intent of the fourth commandment?

A way to sidestep the full and clear intent of the fourth commandment is to liberally interpret two passages from the New Testament, which have been used to essentially nullify this commandment. These are in Matthew 12:1–8 and Galatians 3:13–15:

At that time Jesus went through the grainfields on the Sabbath. His disciples were hungry and began to pick some heads of grain and eat them. When the Pharisees saw this, they said to him, "Look! Your disciples are doing what is unlawful on the Sabbath." He answered, "Haven't you read what David did when he and his companions were hungry? He entered the house of God, and he and his companions ate the consecrated bread—which was not lawful for them to do, but only for the priests. Or haven't you read in the Law that the priests on Sabbath duty in the temple desecrate the Sabbath and yet are innocent? I tell you that something greater than the temple is here. If you had known what these words mean, 'I desire mercy, not sacrifice,' you would not have condemned the innocent. For the Son of Man is Lord of the Sabbath." (Matthew 12:1–8 NIV)

Christ redeemed us from the curse of the law by becoming a curse for us, for it is written: "Cursed is everyone who is hung on a pole." He redeemed us in order that the blessing given to Abraham might come to the Gentiles through Christ Jesus, so that by faith we might receive the promise of the Spirit. Brothers and sisters, let me take an example from everyday life. Just as no one can set aside or add to a human covenant that has been duly established, so it is in this case. (Galatians 3:13–15 NIV)

In Galatians, Paul introduces a new concept, which is Christ "redeemed" us from the curse of the law, the Ten Commandments. That means we can freely break any or all of the Commandments with no consequences, because all of our sins are covered by God's blood sacrifice. So, God has changed from the Old Testament, which holds us responsible for the sins that we choose to commit, by our God-given free will. This is an extremely radical change in God's position on sinfulness and personal responsibility. Is this again one of those situations where something is simply just too good to be true?

Resting on the Sabbath does not mean that you should stay in bed all day. It means that for one day each week, you shall not work for wages and you shall not pay others to serve or work for you. I have thought about those Christian folks whose jobs require them to work on Sunday. This may include hotel staff members, waiters, nurses, doctors, and so on. They will be fired if they don't show up for their scheduled work shift on Sunday. Hopefully, in those cases, they don't work seven days a week, every week. People could choose their Sabbath to be a day of the week when they are scheduled to be off. After all, the Sabbath for Jews is on Saturday; and for Christians, it is on Sunday. There seems to be flexibility as to who determines which day of the week is your Sabbath. Today, good labor practices realize that you need at least one or two days off, each seven-day workweek, to relax and recover from your labors. Do you think that God already knew we needed at least one day of rest for each seven-day week?

You may ask yourself, "What do I do on the Sabbath when I travel on business or go on a vacation?" When we travel out of our hometowns, we are required to pay for food and lodging, even on the Sabbath. God, being perfect, addresses this point; He uses the words "residing in your towns." So paying for these services while on travel does not put you in violation of this law.

You can decide if a medical or other emergency situation, which requires professional services on the Sabbath, would be a violation of the fourth commandment by reading Luke 14:

> One Sabbath, when Jesus went to eat in the house of a prominent Pharisee, he was being carefully watched. There in front of him was a man suffering from abnormal swelling of his body. Jesus asked the Pharisees and experts in the law, "Is it lawful to heal on the Sabbath or not?" But they remained silent. So taking hold of the man, he healed him

and sent him on his way. Then he asked them, "If one of you has a child or an ox that falls into a well on the Sabbath day, will you not immediately pull it out?" And they had nothing to say. (Luke 14:1–6 NIV)

In Matthew 22:34–40, Jesus is asked which commandment is the most important. If He says one commandment is more important than others, that means that the other commandments are less important. If even one commandment is less important than the others, then there is a gray area, where breaking that commandment may not be as sinful. Jesus intentionally didn't answer this question but still gave the perfect response.

> Hearing that Jesus had silenced the Sadducees, the Pharisees got together. One of them, an expert in the law, tested him with this question: "Teacher, which is the greatest Commandment in the Law?" Jesus replied: "'Love the Lord your God with all your heart and with all your soul and with all your mind.' This is the first and greatest Commandment. And the second is like it: 'Love your neighbor as yourself.' All the Law and the Prophets hang on these two Commandments." (Matthew 22:34–40 NIV)

In Mark 12:28–34, Jesus was asked the same question, and He gave essentially the same perfect response. I use the word *essentially* on purpose to point out a subtle but important difference in His replies:

> One of the teachers of the law came and heard them debating. Noticing that Jesus had given them a good answer, he asked Him, "Of all the Commandments, which is the most important?" "The most important one," answered Jesus, "is this: 'Hear, O Israel: The Lord our God, the Lord is one. Love the Lord your God with **all your heart** and

with **all your soul** and with **all your mind** and with **all your strength**.' The second is this: 'Love your neighbor as yourself.' There is no Commandment greater than these." "Well said, Teacher," the man replied. "You are right in saying that God is one and there is no other but Him. To love Him with all your heart, with all your understanding and with all your strength, and to love your neighbor as yourself is more important than all burnt offerings and sacrifices." When Jesus saw that he had answered wisely, He said to him, "You are not far from the kingdom of God." And from then on no one dared ask him any more questions. (Mark 12:28–34 NIV, bold added)

In Matthew, you are to love God with all your heart, soul, and mind, but in Mark, you must also love God with all your strength. This difference doesn't make Matthew wrong, and both are correct. It is just that Mark's account is more complete. What exactly does it mean to love the Lord with all your strength? Strength is demonstrated by some physical action or by the ability to withstand an applied force. A weightlifter's strength is measured by determining the maximum weight that can be lifted. Here, strength is measured by how much work can be accomplished. The strength of a bridge is measured by how much weight it can uphold without failing. To love God with all your strength takes both your good works and upholding God's laws by choosing to obey His commandments. Both your actions and inactions demonstrate your loving obedience to God.

You wish for your children to be obedient and obey your rules, to keep them safe and to make them better people. After all, you are trying to do what is best for your children, by setting limits on them and by guiding their action. You tell your children to look both ways before crossing a street and tell them not to stay out too late. You insist your children study and do their homework, so they learn what is needed to help them succeed in school. But it seems that all children, at some time or another, disobey their parents. Why is this? When children disobey their parents, doesn't it seem like they no longer respect the rules the parents have given them? Don't you respect the ones you truly love? When children have a favorite teacher, one they admire and respect, they will follow the rules, will do all the assigned work, and may even do extra-credit work. If your children love and respect you, don't you think they will obey you?

If you truly love God, shouldn't you respect and obey each and every one of His commandments with all your heart, soul, mind, and strength? After all, isn't God, our Father, giving you laws to keep you safe and to make you a better person as you mature?

Your actions speak louder than words and are much louder than merely thinking about doing something. Do you truly believe it's the thought that counts? James further explains this in James 1:22–25 and James 2:15–19.

> **Do not merely listen to the word, and so deceive yourselves. Do what it says. Anyone who listens to the word but does not do what it says is like someone who looks at his face in a mirror and, after looking at himself, goes away and immediately forgets what he looks like.** But whoever looks intently into the perfect law that gives freedom, and continues in it—not forgetting what they have heard, but doing it—they will be blessed in what they do. (James 1:22–25 NIV, bold added)

> Suppose a brother or a sister is without clothes and daily food. **If one of you says to them, "Go in peace; keep warm and well fed," but does nothing about their physical needs, what good is it?** In the same way, faith by itself, if it is not accompanied by action, is dead. But someone will say, "You have faith; I have deeds." **Show me your faith without deeds, and I will show you my faith by my deeds.** (James 2:15–19 NIV, bold added)

Consider God's seventh commandment, in Exodus 20:14: "You shall not commit adultery." (NIV) Adultery has been defined as consensual sexual intercourse between a married person and another person to whom he/she is not married. However, the word **adulterate** has a much broader meaning that includes making something poorer in quality by adding something else of lessor quality, such as watering down liquor. To adulterate something includes making it impure, degraded, debased, diluted or defiled.

There are five passages in the Bible where a group of people, (nation or generation) are referred to as "adulterous," these include James 4:1-4, Ezekiel 6:9, Matthew 12:38-40, Matthew 16:1-4 and Mark 8:38.

> What causes fights and quarrels among you? Don't they come from your desires that battle within you? You desire but do not have, so you kill. You covet but you cannot get what you want, so you quarrel and fight. You do not have because you do not ask God. When you ask, you do not receive, because you ask with wrong motives, that you may spend what you get on your pleasures. You **adulterous people**, don't you know that friendship with the world means enmity against God? Therefore, **anyone who chooses to be a friend of the world becomes an enemy of God**. (James 4:1–4 NIV, bold added)

> Then in the nations where they have been carried captive, those who escape will remember Me—how I have been grieved by their **adulterous hearts**, which have turned away from Me, and by their eyes, which have lusted after their idols. They will loathe themselves for the evil they have done and for all their detestable practices. (Ezekiel 6:9 NIV, bold added)

Then some of the Pharisees and teachers of the law said to him, "Teacher, we want to see a sign from you." He answered, "A wicked and **adulterous generation** asks for a sign! But none will be given it except the sign of the prophet Jonah. For as Jonah was three days and three nights in the belly of a huge fish, so the Son of Man will be three days and three nights in the heart of the earth. (Matthew 12:38–40 NIV, bold added)

The Pharisees and Sadducees came to Jesus and tested him by asking him to show them a sign from heaven. He replied, "When evening comes, you say, 'It will be fair weather, for the sky is red,' and in the morning, 'Today it will be stormy, for the sky is red and overcast.' You know how to interpret the appearance of the sky, but you cannot interpret the signs of the times. A wicked and **adulterous generation** looks for a sign, but none will be given it except the sign of Jonah." Jesus then left them and went away. (Matthew 16:1–4 NIV, bold added)

If anyone is ashamed of me and my words in this **adulterous and sinful generation**, the Son of Man will be ashamed of them when he comes in his Father's glory with the holy angels." (Mark 8:38 NIV, bold added)

In each of these passages, *adulterous* applies to a group of people and not to an adulterer in the sense of extramarital sex. The term *adulterous* carries a broader meaning of people whose desires or actions are impure or adulterated. Could it be that the seventh commandment not only tells us to not have sex outside the bonds of marriage but also commands us to not adulterate ourselves by being focused on earthly matters instead of seeking righteousness?

CHAPTER 4

WHAT IS GOD-GIVEN WISDOM, AND HOW DO YOU GET IT?

When we pray, we pray for many things. We all hope, wish, or pray for health, healing, friends, financial improvement, love being returned, success, peace, a good night's sleep, and so on. God alone knows each and every one of our thoughts, internal hopes, and desires. Each one of our thoughts might be a prayer to God, with the hope that He will answer them all. God does answer each and every prayer that we ask, but often, God's answer to our prayer is no. God's answers of no are still His perfect answers, even if we don't understand or like His negative responses.

There is one prayer that God will always answer with a yes, which is your sincere prayer for heavenly wisdom. In James 1:5–8, it clearly states that heavenly wisdom is given freely to anyone who trusts in God.

If any of you lacks wisdom, you should ask God, Who gives generously to all without finding fault, and it will be given to you. But when you ask, you must believe and not doubt, because the one who doubts is like a wave of the sea, blown and tossed by the wind. That person should not expect to receive anything from the Lord. Such a person is double-minded and unstable in all they do. (James 1:5–8 NIV, bold added)

The promise is to those who trust in God, even sinners, and whoever asks Him for wisdom will receive it. What is not certain is how quickly your prayers for wisdom will be answered. The answer to a sincere prayer for heavenly wisdom may come in a few minutes, or it may take days, weeks, or even years. Just don't give up on your expectation that God will make you grow in wisdom over time. You must be persistent in your quest for your God-given wisdom. Chapter 7 of this book addresses patience and perseverance, while you wait for heavenly wisdom.

You probably know of people who can memorize a lot of facts and data about a few specific topics. These people may be outstanding in their field and may be well compensated for their knowledge. But is such factual knowledge equal to Godly or heavenly wisdom? Some people may have an advanced college degree but lack the common sense to function well in daily life. Some have very little formal education, yet they are clever or creative enough to be multimillionaires. James 3:13–18 clarifies that there are two kinds of wisdom: earthly and heavenly. James also lays out the personal characteristics that grow stronger in a person with heavenly wisdom. These are characteristics that a person needs to walk the narrow path of righteousness.

Who is wise and understanding among you? Let them show it by their good life, by deeds done in the humility that comes from [heavenly] wisdom. But if you harbor bitter envy and selfish ambition in your hearts, do not boast about it or deny the truth. **Such "wisdom" does not come down from heaven but is earthly, unspiritual, demonic.** For where you have envy and selfish ambition, there you find disorder and every evil practice. But the wisdom that comes from heaven is first of all pure; then peace-loving, considerate, submissive, full of mercy and good fruit, impartial and sincere. Peacemakers who sow in peace reap a harvest of righteousness. (James 3:13 NIV, **bold added**)

The story of God giving Solomon wisdom, found in 1 Kings 3 and 4, is very interesting and worth repeating:

At Gibeon the LORD appeared to Solomon during the night in a dream, and God said, "Ask for whatever you want me to give you." Solomon answered, "You have shown great kindness to your servant, my father David, because he was faithful to you and righteous and upright in heart. You have continued this great kindness to him and have given him a son to sit on his throne this very day. Now, LORD my God, you have made your servant king in place of my father David. But I am only a little child and do not know how to carry out my duties. Your servant is here among the people you have chosen, a great people, too numerous to count or number. So give your servant a discerning heart to govern your people and to distinguish between right and wrong. For who is able to govern this great people of yours?" The Lord was pleased that Solomon had asked for this. So God said to him, "Since you have asked for this and not for long life or wealth for yourself, nor have asked for the death of your enemies but for discernment in administering justice, I will do what you have asked. I will give you a wise and discerning heart, so that there will never have been anyone like you, nor will there ever be. Moreover, I will give you what you have not asked for—both wealth and honor—so that in your lifetime you will have no equal among kings. And if you walk in obedience to Me and keep My decrees and commands as David your father did, I will give you a long life." (1 Kings 3:5–14 NIV)

> God gave Solomon wisdom and very great insight, and a breadth of understanding as measureless as the sand on the seashore. Solomon's wisdom was greater than the wisdom of all the people of the East, and greater than all the wisdom of Egypt. He was wiser than anyone else, including Ethan the Ezrahite—wiser than Heman, Kalkol and Darda, the sons of Mahol. And his fame spread to all the surrounding nations. He spoke three thousand proverbs and his songs numbered a thousand and five. He spoke about plant life, from the cedar of Lebanon to the hyssop that grows out of walls. He also spoke about animals and birds, reptiles and fish. From all nations people came to listen to Solomon's wisdom, sent by all the kings of the world, who had heard of his wisdom. (1 Kings 4:29–34 NIV)

After you pray for wisdom, only God knows when you will receive it. The Bible helps you as to where you can find heavenly wisdom. After all, you certainly can't get it from local wise guys or buy it in a store. Assistance to help you in your search for this wisdom can be found in Job 28:12–13 and 28:17–28:

> But where can wisdom be found? Where does understanding dwell? No mortal comprehends its worth; it cannot be found in the land of the living. (Job 28:12–13 NIV)

> Neither gold nor crystal can compare with it [wisdom], nor can it be had for jewels of gold. Coral and jasper are not worthy of mention; the price of wisdom is beyond rubies. The topaz of Cush cannot compare with it; **it cannot be bought with pure gold. Where then does wisdom come from?** Where does understanding dwell? It is hidden from

the eyes of every living thing, concealed even from the birds in the sky. Destruction and Death say, "Only a rumor of it has reached our ears." **God understands the way to it [wisdom,] and He alone knows where it dwells,** for He views the ends of the earth and sees everything under the heavens. When He established the force of the wind and measured out the waters, when He made a decree for the rain and a path for the thunderstorm, then He looked at wisdom and appraised it; He confirmed it and tested it. And He said to the human race, "**The fear of the Lord—that is wisdom, and to shun evil is understanding.**" (Job 28:17–28 NIV, bold added)

The Bible also helps to identify where wisdom *cannot* be found, specifically again in the book of Job. Here, Elihu says he will teach Job about wisdom, but in fact, Elihu is a liar. God affirms that Job's friends were not speaking the truth:

After the LORD had said these things to Job, he said to Eliphaz the Temanite, "I am angry with you and your two friends, because you have not spoken the truth about Me, as My servant Job has." (Job 42:7 NIV)

Elihu's false teachings about wisdom are introduced in Job 33:1–4 and 31–33. Elihu's wisdom condemns Job as being a wicked man and lies about Job's righteousness, in Job 34:35 and 37. And just like Job's "friends," Elihu repeats what they say, that wicked people will reap what they sow while on earth, for example in Job 4:8.

But now, Job, listen to my words; pay attention to everything I say. I am about to open my mouth; my words are on the tip of my tongue. My words come from an upright heart; my lips sincerely speak what I know. The Spirit of God has made me; the breath of the Almighty gives me life. (Job 33:1–4)

Pay attention, Job, and listen to me; be silent, and I will speak. If you have anything to say, answer me; speak up, for I want to vindicate you. But if not, then listen to me; be silent, and I will teach you wisdom. (Job 33:31–33 NIV)

'Job speaks without knowledge; his words lack insight.' Oh, that Job might be tested to the utmost for answering like a wicked man! To his sin he adds rebellion; scornfully he claps his hands among us and multiplies his words against God. (Job 34:35–36 NIV)

As I have observed, those who plow evil and those who sow trouble reap it. (Job 4:8 NIV)

So what have we learned about how to gain God-given heavenly wisdom?

1. God will freely give us wisdom, regardless of our faults, when we sincerely ask Him for it.
2. God can be completely trusted to give us His wisdom.
3. We must be patient and persevere, while waiting to gain His heavenly wisdom.
4. False wisdom may be offered by those close to you.
5. Heavenly wisdom may come in ways that may not be anticipated.
6. Fear of the Lord is the first gift of heavenly wisdom.

CHAPTER 5

DOES GOD TEMPT YOU, AND WHERE DOES TEMPTATION LEAD YOU?

Asking if God tempts us and how we are tempted raises the fundamental question about how can we be led astray. How are we led off the straight and narrow path, leading to heaven, and onto a sinful path that leads to our damnation? In the first chapter of James, he says: "When tempted, no one should say, 'God is tempting me.' For God cannot be tempted by evil, **nor does He tempt anyone.**" (James 1:13 NIV, bold added)

This raises a question about the Lord's Prayer. The Lord's Prayer originates from both Matthew 6:9–13 and Luke 11:2–4, which are combined to make what is also called the Our Father Prayer.

> This, then, is how you should pray: "Our Father in heaven, hallowed be your name, your kingdom come, your will be done, on earth as it is in heaven. Give us today our daily bread. And forgive us our debts, as we also have forgiven

our debtors. **And lead us not into temptation**, but deliver us from the evil one." (Matthew 6:9–13 NIV, bold added)

He said to them, "When you pray, say: 'Father, hallowed be your name, your kingdom come. Give us each day our daily bread. Forgive us our sins, for we also forgive everyone who sins against us. **And lead us not into temptation**.'" (Luke 11:2–4 NIV, bold added)

Why would or should we pray for God not to lead us into temptation? Why would He lead us into temptation? Wouldn't that be like leading His flock to slaughter? James 4:5 (NIV) says, "Do you think Scripture says without reason that He jealously longs for the spirit He has caused to dwell in us?" God, Who wants us to love Him, would never lead us into temptation, which can lead to sin, damnation, and ultimate separation from God Himself. Leading us into temptation seems to be a job much more suited for demonic beings.

Most Protestants add to the end of the Lord's Prayer the phrase: "For Thine is the kingdom and the power and the glory forever and ever. Amen." Catholics do not add this phrase. Also, some use the word *trespasses* as a synonym for sins or debts. After people have made such subtle changes to the Lord's Prayer, is it okay to say a more positive prayer to God to lead us away from temptation? God can surely do this by giving us His heavenly wisdom.

Additionally, about being led into temptation, James 1:13–18 (NIV) says the following.

When tempted, no one should say, "God is tempting me." For God cannot be tempted by evil, nor does He tempt anyone; but **each person is tempted when they are dragged away by their own evil desire and enticed. Then, after desire has conceived, it gives birth to sin; and sin, when it is full-grown, gives birth to death.** Don't be deceived, my dear brothers and sisters. Every good and perfect gift is from above, coming down from the Father of the heavenly lights, Who does not change like shifting shadows. He chose to give us birth through the word of truth, that we might be a kind of firstfruits of all he created.

The seeds of sin are your own self-serving desires and inactions, lustfulness, greed, envy, and coveting what others have. These seeds grow into producing sins, which sets you on your highway to hell. This is truly not the path that God desires you to follow, so as to gain your heavenly reward. James further clarifies the idea of earthly desires as being the seeds of sinfulness:

> Religion that God our Father accepts as pure and faultless is this: to look after orphans and widows in their distress and to **keep oneself from being polluted by the world.** (James 1:27 NIV, bold added)

> For where you have **envy and selfish ambition, there you find disorder and every evil practice.** But the wisdom that comes from heaven is first of all pure; then peace-loving, considerate, submissive, full of mercy and good fruit, impartial and sincere. Peacemakers who sow in peace reap a harvest of righteousness. (James 3:16–18 NIV, bold added)

> What causes fights and quarrels among you? **Don't they come from your desires that battle within you? You desire but do not have, so you kill. You covet but you cannot get what you want, so you quarrel and fight. You do not have because you do not ask God. When you ask, you do not receive, because you ask with wrong motives, that you may spend what you get on your pleasures. You adulterous people, don't you know that friendship with the world means enmity against God? Therefore,**

anyone who chooses to be a friend of the world becomes an enemy of God. Or do you think scripture says without reason that he jealously longs for the spirit he has caused to dwell in us? But he gives us more grace. That is why scripture says: "God opposes the proud but shows favor to the humble." Submit yourselves, then, to God. Resist the devil, and he will flee from you. Come near to God and he will come near to you. **Wash your hands, you sinners, and purify your hearts, you double-minded.** Grieve, mourn and wail. Change your laughter to mourning and your joy to gloom. Humble yourselves before the Lord, and he will lift you up. (James 4:1–10 NIV, bold added)

You should rein in and control your thought processes, which lead you to temptation. This is one of your first steps on your path to salvation. The importance of controlling your thoughts, which lead you to sin, is also expressed in Proverbs 6:20–25 and Mathew 15:15–20:

My son, keep your father's command and do not forsake your mother's teaching. Bind them always on your heart; fasten them around your neck. When you walk, they will guide you; when you sleep, they will watch over you; when you awake, they will speak to you. For this command is a lamp, this teaching is a light, and correction and instruction are the way to life, keeping you from your neighbor's wife, from the smooth talk of a wayward woman. **Do not lust in your heart after her beauty** or let her captivate you with her eyes. (Proverbs 6:20–25 NIV, bold added)

Peter said, "Explain the parable to us." "Are you still so dull?" Jesus asked them. "Don't you see that whatever enters the mouth goes into the stomach and then out of the body? But the things that come out of a person's mouth come from the heart, and these defile them. **For out of the heart come evil thoughts—murder, adultery, sexual immorality, theft, false testimony, slander. These are what defile a person; but eating with unwashed hands does not defile them."** (Mathew 15:15–20 NIV, bold added)

Does God lead us into temptation, or is it earthly or demonic desire that leads us into temptation? When we are approaching any of the many paths into temptation, we must not think about or rationalize our heading into that direction. God longs for your righteousness, and He will help you to resist the devil by giving you the heavenly wisdom you need to choose the correct path. He does this when you ask Him sincerely for His wisdom, even if you have gone down some wrong paths before.

CHAPTER 6

How Is Facing Trials Good for You?

A doctor once told me about illnesses, if it doesn't kill you; it will make you stronger, which is similar to what Friedrich Nietzsche said, "That which does not kill us makes us stronger." It's an old but true saying; your body develops an immunity to a disease, if you survive it. God designs your body to fight a disease with fevers, vomiting, and activating your immune system. It may be a painful process, but you come out immune to a disease, after your body has defeated it. The same concept applies to your spiritual health. If you face a temptation and persevere against sinning, won't you become stronger to resist more temptations in the future? Even if you fail and sin, you can take the lessons learned from your errors, to ask for forgiveness and for the wisdom to not repeat the same sins again.

James says that your trials and hardships should be enjoyed. This may not seem like the case while you are suffering, but you will be better after the experience. It's not just enjoying that your trial has finally ended, but also cherish the lessons learned during your trial. The strongest lessons you can learn are those you learned first-hand, the hard way. But also take the advice of others, from their lessons learned, to help you on the straight and narrow path. A good example of this is listening to and applying the wisdom given to you by your parents and elders, who have lived a few years and can teach you from their experience. The first chapter of James discusses this:

> **Consider it pure joy, my brothers and sisters, whenever you face trials of many kinds**, because you know that the testing of your faith produces perseverance. Let perseverance finish its work so that you may be mature and complete, not lacking anything. (James 1:2–4 NIV, bold added)

> **Blessed is the one who perseveres under trial** because, having stood the test, that person will receive the crown of life that the Lord has promised to those who love Him. (James 1:12 NIV, bold added)

Job is the perfect example of perseverance under extremely harsh trials. The first of Job's many trials is that all his children and most of his servants are killed and all his livestock is stolen or killed. But Job perseveres and says that God both gives and takes and that he still praises God. Next Job is afflicted with painful diseases, almost to the point of death. All of Job's friends and acquaintances turn on him and mock him and tell him lies about God's vengeance being cast upon him, because he is wicked and evil. Despite all this, Job still praises the Lord.

Have you ever met people who, when extreme troubles happen in their lives, turn away from God or stop praising or trusting the Lord? People can pray with perfectly good intentions and motives, but God's answer can still be no. An answer of no from God may not be the answer you hoped for, but it's still His answer. It is beyond our understanding why God answers yes, no, or later to our prayers, but regardless of how the Lord answers your prayers, don't let that damage your trust in Him. If you disrespect His negative answers to your prayers, who do you think you are?

Your physical trials and the testing of your faith may seem

unending, just as they seemed to Job. But all your trials will absolutely end someday. You should look at your eternal goal, not just at what may happen to you today, tomorrow, or a few years in the future. Throughout your hard times, stay faithful and continually praise God. I had a close friend who died of extremely painful bone cancer; his agony was horrific. He told me he didn't mind the pain so much, except he hated to see his wife and children watch him suffer. He was a truly a perfect example of an unselfish and loving husband and father. He withstood his trials, even to death, and still remained a strong believer and a man of God. Hopefully, all of us can be this faithful and loving in the good and bad times and even worse times that we may face.

The trials and suffering of Job and his perseverance during his bad times are discussed further in the next chapter. In Job 2:9–10 (NIV), Job knows that we are subject to good times and to very bad times in our lives. He accepts this fact that we may suffer greatly in our life on earth:

> His wife said to him, "Are you still maintaining your integrity? Curse God and die!" He replied, "You are talking like a foolish woman. Shall we accept good from God, and not trouble?" In all this, Job did not sin in what he said.

Being under trials can make or break a person, physically, mentally, or spiritually. We should not focus on surviving our trials in the physical sense. Physical trials, like disease or old age, will ultimately lead to death; that's a trial no one ever overcomes. But your spirit can and will survive by having a more complete, open, and growing trust in God, during your good times, bad times and trials. Again, if bad things happen, you should let them make you stronger, make you wiser, and help you grow more in your trust in the Lord.

CHAPTER 7

WHAT ABOUT PATIENCE AND PERSEVERANCE?

You may hear someone has the patience of Job. Patience is simply having the ability to wait for something to occur; like waiting for the water to boil, getting your car repaired, getting your paycheck on Friday, or opening gifts on Christmas. Job had more perseverance than patience, because he suffered greatly over a long time, but he didn't fail in his suffering, by cursing God. James 5:7–12 (NIV) discusses both patience and perseverance:

> Be patient, then, brothers and sisters, until the Lord's coming. See how the farmer waits for the land to yield its valuable crop, patiently waiting for the autumn and spring rains. You too, be patient and stand firm, because the Lord's coming is near. Don't grumble against one another, brothers and sisters, or you will be judged. The Judge is standing at the door! Brothers and sisters, as an example of patience in the face of suffering, take the prophets who spoke in the name of the Lord. As you know, we count as blessed those who have persevered. You have heard of Job's perseverance

and have seen what the Lord finally brought about. The Lord is full of compassion and mercy.

The prophets of the Old Testament foretold of the coming of Jesus Christ in many ways, by predicting the multitude of signs that would be fulfilled when our Savior arrives. None of these prophets lived to see the day when Christ is born. These prophets persevered their entire lifetime waiting for this miracle; and isn't a lifetime of waiting a great example of true and faithful patience and perseverance? Be patient; the Lord is coming soon, because the moment your earthly body dies, that is the day you will meet the Lord. How quickly will that occur? Probably, sooner than any of us would wish for.

Perseverance is a major theme in the book of Job; however, many additional points may be missed, perhaps because this book of Job is so long. One very important point is that Job was a righteous man. In the King James Version (KJV) of the Bible, there is a strong statement about Job's righteousness in Job 1:1. God reaffirms this assessment of Job in verses 1:6–8:

> There was a man in the land of Uz, whose name was Job; and that man was **perfect** and upright, and one that feared God, and eschewed evil. (Job 1:1 KJV, bold added)

> One day the angels came to present themselves before the LORD, and Satan also came with them. The LORD said to Satan, "Where have you come from?" Satan answered the LORD, "From roaming throughout the earth, going back and forth on it." Then the LORD said to Satan, "Have you considered my servant Job? There is no one on earth like him; **he is blameless and upright**, a man who fears God and shuns evil." (Job 1:6–8 NIV, bold added)

Other English translations of God's description of Job all

conclude that he is a righteous man. Examples of these translations follow:

- a perfect and an upright man, one that feareth God, and escheweth evil (King James Version)
- a perfect and an upright man, one that feareth God, and abstaineth from evil (The Darby Translation)
- a man without sin and upright, fearing God and keeping himself far from evil (The Bible in Basic English)
- a man of perfect integrity, who fears God and turns away from evil (Holman Christian Standard Bible)
- a blameless and upright man who fears God and shuns evil (The Complete Jewish Bible)
- a man who is honest, who is of absolute integrity, who reveres God and avoids evil (Common English Bible)
- a perfect and an upright man, one that feareth God, and turneth away from evil (American Standard Version)
- He is a man of integrity: He is decent, he fears God, and he stays away from evil (GOD'S WORD Translation)
- He worships Me and is careful not to do anything evil (Good News Translation)
- a blameless and upright man, who fears God and turns away from evil (English Standard Version)
- He is blameless—a man of complete integrity. He fears God and stays away from evil (New Living Translation)

In the first chapter of Job, God brings up Job's name to Satan, which means He anticipated Satan's next move. Satan then makes a wager with God in Job 1:9–11 (NIV), saying that Job will curse God, if all that Job possesses and has been blessed with is taken away from him.

> "Does Job fear God for nothing?" Satan replied. "Have You not put a hedge around him and his household and

everything he has? You have blessed the work of his hands, so that his flocks and herds are spread throughout the land. But now stretch out Your hand and strike everything he has, and he will surely curse You to Your face."

God, being omniscient (all knowing), already knows the outcome of this bet, and He accepts Satan's wager in Job 1:12 (NIV): "The LORD said to Satan, 'Very well, then, everything he has is in your power, but on the man himself do not lay a finger.' Then Satan went out from the presence of the LORD."

After Job's livestock is stolen or killed, most of his servants are killed, and all his sons and daughters are killed, Job still does not curse God and continues to praise the name of the Lord, knowing that God both gives and takes away.

In chapter 2 of Job, Satan ups the ante of his wager with God. Satan says that if Job is tortured to the brink of death, then Job will surely curse God to His face. During Job's tortures, it's important to point out that the people who talk to and lecture Job are telling him half-truths and lies. (Job 42:7) These "friends" try to convince Job that he is being punished for his sins: "Those who plow evil and those who sow trouble shall] reap it." (Job 4:8 NIV) They also tell Job that his children are evil:"When your children sinned against Him, He gave them over to the penalty of their sin" (Job 8:4 NIV) These people are doing the work of Satan, by lecturing and tormenting Job in order to lead him into cursing God. Even Job's wife shared in this chorus of taunting:

> His wife said to him, "Are you still maintaining your integrity? Curse God and die!" (Job: 2:9 NIV)

Job's tormentors say that if a person is evil, God will punish him while he's alive. Unfortunately, this misconception is repeated many times by Job's friends. In Job 18:1–21, Bildad lists the many earthly curses that a wicked man will experience, and later, Elipaz attacks Job's character:

> What pleasure would it give the Almighty if you were righteous? What would He gain if your ways were blameless? Is it for your piety that He rebukes you and brings charges against you? **Is not your wickedness great? Are not your sins endless?** (Job 22:3–5 NIV, bold added)

Nevertheless, after every attack on Job's righteousness and character, he resists and refutes their lies with the truth. He further explains that God may not punish a wicked person while they are still alive, in Job 21:7–14. A modern example of a wicked man who spent his years in prosperity, and died at the old age of seventy-four, is Joseph Stalin, the dictator of the Soviet Union for thirty years. In the 1930s, he killed at least seven hundred thousand enemies of the state and imprisoned over a million people, in what is called the Great Purge.

> **Why do the wicked live on, growing old and increasing in power?** They see their children established around them, their offspring before their eyes. Their homes are safe and free from fear; the rod of God is not on them. Their bulls never fail to breed; their cows calve and do not miscarry. They send forth their children as a flock; their little ones dance about. They sing to the music of timbrel [tambourine] and lyre; they make merry to the sound of the pipe. **They spend their years in prosperity and go down to the grave in peace.** Yet they say to God, 'Leave us alone! We have no desire to know your ways. (Job 21:7–14 NIV, bold added)

Still while in his tremendous suffering, Job says, "Though He slay me, yet will I hope in Him; I will surely defend my ways to His face." (Job 13:15 NIV) Later, he says:

But He knows the way that I take; when He has tested me, I will come forth as gold. My feet have closely followed His steps; I have kept to His way without turning aside. I have not departed from the commands of His lips; I have treasured the words of His mouth more than my daily bread. (Job 23:10–12 NIV)

After Job's perseverance through all of his losses, suffering and listening to untruthful lectures, God restores more than what Job had lost and blesses him with seven sons and three daughters. (Job 42:7–17) It is interesting that Job's three daughters are named, while his sons are not named. It also says that his daughters are beautiful and are granted an inheritance along with his sons.

The book of Job not only has the great lesson of perseverance; it has much more, because it tells of how people lie about God and about how He operates. Have you ever heard a person using words that sound godly but are actually demonic? With God-given wisdom, you can determine what is true and what is not.

CHAPTER 8

ARE YOU RICH? DO YOU SHOW FAVORITISM?

Do you think of yourself as being rich or poor? Rich is a term that is relative and subject to your own feelings and circumstances. I don't feel that I am rich, especially when compared to millionaires and billionaires. On the other hand, the vast majority of people who live in underdeveloped countries may consider those who live in the United States, like me, to be like millionaires. Most all of us have running water, indoor plumbing, electricity, refrigeration, and television. All of these are conveniences available to us 24/7. In planning a business trip to Uganda, one of the hotels proudly proclaimed they had electricity twenty-four hours a day. Many of the homes there are without electricity, and people have to haul in five-gallon containers of kerosene to light their homes and cook their food. The unemployment rate in Uganda is at 40 percent, and there is no government assistance for these unemployed people. These poor souls must rely on their family, friends, and neighbors for food and shelter. But 60 percent of Ugandans are employed and much better off than those who are unemployed. By comparison to others, do you need to consider yourself rich?

James has several things to say about the rich and the poor, starting with James 1:9–11 (NIV):

> Believers in humble circumstances ought to take pride in their high position. But the rich should take pride in their humiliation—since they will pass away like a wild flower. For the sun rises with scorching heat and withers the plant; its blossom falls and its beauty is destroyed. In the same way, the rich will fade away even while they go about their business.

The entire lifetime of a wildflower is a single season, while your lifetime will span a number of years. James is not saying the rich will fade away within a year, but they certainly have a life that will surely end. In James 5:1–6 (NIV), he further discusses wealthy people:

> Now listen, you rich people, weep and wail because of the misery that is coming on you. Your wealth has rotted, and moths have eaten your clothes. Your gold and silver are corroded. Their corrosion will testify against you and eat your flesh like fire. You have hoarded wealth in the last days. Look! The wages you failed to pay the workers who mowed your fields are crying out against you. The cries of the harvesters have reached the ears of the Lord Almighty. You have lived on earth in luxury and self-indulgence. You have fattened yourselves in the day of slaughter. You have condemned and murdered the innocent one, who was not opposing you.

Another way to say all this is that the hearse that you ride in to your funeral does not come with a luggage rack, to carry your worldly possessions to your grave. And if your wealth is ill-gotten, the abuses you committed to gain that money will ultimately be held against you by God.

These and other Biblical passages are clear on how the desire for, the love of, or even the worship of money, gold, and wealth can corrupt and cause you to stray off the narrow path that God wants you to follow to your heavenly reward. Some preachers today quote scriptures, perhaps out of context, about how God wants you to prosper and have an abundant live. But if you take their words to mean you should unfairly take another's money, you are heading down the path to damnation.

Matthew 19:24, Mark 10:25, and Luke 18:25 all have a similar message: "It is easier for a camel to go through the eye of a needle than for someone who is rich to enter the kingdom of God." Here, Jesus is not referring to the eye of a sewing needle. The eye of a needle is the name of very small gate in the wall around a city, like Jerusalem's Eye of the Needle, which is still there today. It is built in such a way as to prevent marauders mounted on horses from entering the city. This eye of a needle gate remains open at night, after the city's main gates are closed. To enter the small gate, a camel's packages must first be removed; and even then, the camel must stoop to be led through such a low and narrow gate.

To give more insight on how difficult it is for a rich person to get into heaven, three Gospels have three similar stories, where Jesus is asked the question, how do you can get into heaven and have eternal life? His answer is not too pleasing to the person asking the question. Matthew 19:16–22 (NIV, bold added) says:

> Just then a man came up to Jesus and asked, "Teacher, what good thing must I do to get eternal life?" "Why do you ask Me about what is good?" Jesus replied. "There is only One Who is good. If you want to enter life, keep the Commandments." "Which ones?" he inquired. Jesus replied, "'You shall not murder, you shall not commit adultery, you shall not steal, you shall not give false testimony, honor your father and mother,' and 'love your neighbor as yourself.' "All these I have kept," the young man said. "What do I

still lack?" Jesus answered, "**If you want to be perfect, go, sell your possessions and give to the poor, and you will have treasure in heaven.** Then come, follow Me." When the young man heard this, he went away sad, because he had great wealth.

Mark 10:17–22 (NIV, bold added) says:

> As Jesus started on his way, a man ran up to him and fell on his knees before him. "Good teacher," he asked, "what must I do to inherit eternal life?" "Why do you call Me good?" Jesus answered. "No one is good—except God alone. You know the Commandments: 'You shall not murder, you shall not commit adultery, you shall not steal, you shall not give false testimony, you shall not defraud [a form of stealing], honor your father and mother.'" "Teacher," he declared, "all these I have kept since I was a boy." Jesus looked at him and loved him. "One thing you lack," he said. "**Go, sell everything you have and give to the poor, and you will have treasure in heaven.** Then come, follow Me." At this the man's face fell. He went away sad, because he had great wealth.

Luke 18:18–23 (NIV, bold added) says:

> A certain ruler asked him, "Good teacher, what must I do to inherit eternal life?" "Why do you call Me good?" Jesus answered. "No one is good—except God alone. You know the Commandments: 'You shall not commit adultery, you shall not murder, you shall not steal, you shall not give false testimony, honor your father and mother.'" "All these I have kept since I was a boy," he said. When Jesus heard this, He said to him, "You still lack one thing. **Sell everything you have and give to the poor, and you will have treasure in**

heaven. Then come, follow Me." When he heard this, he became very sad, because he was very wealthy.

Jesus doesn't say that it's impossible for wealthy people to get into heaven, but it is more difficult for them to get there. These are some constraints that may keep a wealthy person out of heaven:

- loving money to the detriment of others, instead of loving God and practicing His laws
- seeking worldly pleasures, without asking, "What does God want me to do?"
- bragging about your possessions and planning to get more possessions, without wanting to share your good fortunes
- taking less fortunate people to court to gain what is theirs

It may seem like somewhat of a dilemma about being rich and getting into heaven. After all, Job was very wealthy. (See Job 1:3–4) But God still called Job righteous; however, He also said in Job 1:8, (NIV, bold added) "There is **no one on earth like him**; he is blameless and upright, a man who fears God and shuns evil." Job was a one-of-a-kind person, and despite his wealth, he still remained righteous. Couldn't you do this too, with enough perseverance?

It is a bit perplexing that Jesus Christ requires people to sell everything they own and give the money to the poor. As soon as they do this, they become a poor person. Jesus did not set a time frame for this transfer of money to happen; should it be today, next week, or next year? And when all is said and done, everyone will give up all their wealth; as we all know, we can't take it with us. If a wealthy person wrote a will to give everything to charity, would that meet the requirement to get treasures in heaven? What if a person leaves everything to their immediate family, who are poor or at least less wealthy; would that meet the standard that Jesus set?

Also, in the Gospel of Luke, a different standard is set for giving up your possessions to the poor for salvation. Why is giving up only one-half of this man's possession to the poor the key to his salvation?

> But Zacchaeus stood up and said to the Lord, "Look, Lord! Here and now I give **half of my possessions to the poor**, and if I have cheated anybody out of anything, I will pay back four times the amount." Jesus said to him, "**Today salvation has come to this house**, because this man, too, is a son of Abraham. For the Son of Man came to seek and to save the lost." (Luke 19:8–10 NIV, bold added)

Another story about giving to the poor is also brought up in John 12:1–9 (NIV, bold added), which has an interesting twist about giving money to the poor:

> Six days before the Passover, Jesus came to Bethany, where Lazarus lived, whom Jesus had raised from the dead. Here a dinner was given in Jesus' honor. Martha served, while Lazarus was among those reclining at the table with him. Then Mary took about a pint of pure nard, an expensive perfume; she poured it on Jesus' feet and wiped His feet with her hair. And the house was filled with the fragrance of the perfume. But one of His disciples, Judas Iscariot, who was later to betray Him, objected, "Why wasn't this perfume sold and the money given to the poor? It was worth a year's wages." He did not say this because he cared about the poor but because he was a thief; as keeper of the money bag, he used to help himself to what was put into it. "Leave her alone," Jesus replied. "It was intended that she should save this perfume for the day of My burial. **You will always have the poor among you**, but you will not always have Me."

Here are more insights about giving away your money to the church (temple):

Jesus sat down opposite the place where the offerings were put and watched the crowd putting their money into the temple treasury. Many rich people threw in large amounts. [42] But a poor widow came and put in two very small copper coins, worth only a few cents. [43] Calling His disciples to Him, Jesus said, "Truly I tell you, this poor widow has put more into the treasury than all the others. [44] They all gave out of their wealth; but she, out of her poverty, put in everything—all she had to live on." (Mark 12:41–44 NIV)

As Jesus looked up, He saw the rich putting their gifts into the temple treasury. He also saw a poor widow put in two very small copper coins. "Truly I tell you," He said, "this poor widow has put in more than all the others. All these people gave their gifts out of their wealth; but she out of her poverty put in all she had to live on." (Luke 21:2–4 NIV)

Which is more important? How much you give to the poor, or what is in your heart with your generosity towards those less fortunate than yourself? In conclusion, James 2:15–17 (NIV) discusses how more fortunate people should help the poor:

Suppose a brother or a sister is without clothes and daily food. If one of you says to them, "Go in peace; keep warm and well fed," but does nothing about their physical needs, what good is it? In the same way, faith by itself, if it is not accompanied by action, is dead.

Changing subjects somewhat, let's look at how showing favoritism may be a bad idea. Would you be more attentive to a rich person than to a poor person? Is the person dressed in a suit and tie smarter or more trustworthy than the person wearing blue jeans and flip-flops? Are any physical characteristics, such as skin color, height, weight, etc. an indicator of a person's moral character? James 2:1–9 (NIV, bold added) has a lot to say about showing favoritism:

> My brothers and sisters, believers in our glorious Lord Jesus Christ must not show favoritism. Suppose a man comes into your meeting wearing a gold ring and fine clothes, and a poor man in filthy old clothes also comes in. **If you show special attention to the man wearing fine clothes and say, "Here's a good seat for you," but say to the poor man, "You stand there" or "Sit on the floor by my feet," have you not discriminated among yourselves and become judges with evil thoughts?** Listen, my dear brothers and sisters: Has not God chosen those who are poor in the eyes of the world to be rich in faith and to inherit the kingdom he promised those who love him? But you have dishonored the poor. Is it not the rich who are exploiting you? Are they not the ones who are dragging you into court? Are they not the ones who are blaspheming the noble name of Him to whom you belong? If you really keep the royal law found in scripture, "**Love your neighbor as yourself**," you are doing right. **But if you show favoritism, you sin** and are convicted by the law as lawbreakers.

Showing favoritism means you think someone is better or more deserving than another person, and it also shows your disdain for those who you don't favor. The point that we are all God's children is clearly stated in Job 31:13–15 (NIV):

> If I have denied justice to any of my servants, whether male or female, when they had a grievance against me, what will I do when God confronts me? What will I answer when called to account? Did not He Who made me in the womb make them? Did not the same One form us both within our mothers?

Job says that he and other people are the same when being formed in their mother's womb. Should an unborn child have the same respect and rights as any other living human? Aren't the unborn alive with a soul, who must be murdered to terminate a pregnancy?

Each and every person is created equal in the eyes of God, which is considered to be a self-evident truth. We are all exactly the same, with only superficial differences, which will be totally meaningless the second after our death. In the end, it is only your immortal soul that is truly worthwhile. Indeed, you must love everyone exactly the same way you love the wonderful person you are. You are created by God, in His image, and He loves you. Shouldn't you respect everyone, regardless of their circumstances or position of power? Isn't that what God wants you to do?

CHAPTER 9

DO YOU HAVE AN ALLIGATOR MOUTH?

One of the strongest messages contained in James is the importance of controlling what you say to others. James says that angry and disrespectful speech is not the way to express your love for your neighbors. When you become angry and tell someone off or slice and dice them with your words, aren't you essentially saying that you are superior to that person? Don't we all make mistakes? Aren't we all sinners? Aren't we all equal in the eyes of God?

Controlling what you say and how you say it is necessary to deliver effective and constructive criticism. And you need to listen to who you are talking to so you can understand their side of the story and let them know of your concern for their situation. The other person's opinions and decisions are just as important to them as your opinions are to you. Even children, with childish ideas that may be self-destructive, cannot be persuaded to change their ideas by yelling at them in anger. When you see a character acting angry on a TV show or movie, don't you wonder about the stability of that person? You wonder what bad things that character will do.

The book of James goes into great detail to clarify how bad it is to speak words of anger:

My dear brothers and sisters, take note of this: **Everyone should be quick to listen, slow to speak and slow to become angry, because human anger does not produce the righteousness that God desires.** Therefore, get rid of all moral filth and the evil that is so prevalent and humbly accept the word planted in you, which can save you. (James 1:19–21 NIV, bold added)

Those who consider themselves religious and yet do not keep a tight rein on their tongues deceive themselves, and their religion is worthless. (James 1:26 NIV)

Not many of you should become teachers, my fellow believers, because you know that we who teach will be judged more strictly. We all stumble in many ways. **Anyone who is never at fault in what they say is perfect**, able to keep their whole body in check. When we put bits into the mouths of horses to make them obey us, we can turn the whole animal. Or take ships as an example. Although they are so large and are driven by strong winds, they are steered by a very small rudder wherever the pilot wants to go. **Likewise, the tongue is a small part of the body, but it makes great boasts.** Consider what (sic that) a great forest is set on fire by a small spark. **The tongue also is a fire, a world of evil among the parts of the body. It corrupts the whole body, sets the whole course of one's life on fire, and is itself set on fire by hell.** All kinds of animals, birds, reptiles and sea creatures are being tamed and have been tamed by mankind, but **no human being can tame the tongue. It is a restless evil, full of deadly poison. With the tongue we praise our Lord and Father, and with it we curse human beings, who have been made in God's likeness. Out of the same mouth come praise and cursing. My brothers and sisters, this should not**

be. Can both fresh water and salt water flow from the same spring? My brothers and sisters, can a fig tree bear olives; or a grapevine bear figs? Neither can a salt spring produce fresh water. (James 3:1–12 NIV, bold added)

Speaking an oath is also mentioned in James, where he addresses what you need to say when giving sworn testimony. You don't have the power to uphold or back up your oath based on the support of things beyond your control. This is mentioned in James 5:12 and is further explained in Matthew 5:33–37:

> Above all, my brothers and sisters, do not swear—not by heaven or by earth or by anything else. All you need to say is a simple "Yes" or "No." Otherwise you will be condemned. (James 5:12 NIV)

> Again, you have heard that it was said to the people long ago, "Do not break your oath, but fulfill to the Lord the vows you have made." But I tell you, **do not swear an oath at all: either by heaven, for it is God's throne; or by the earth, for it is his footstool; or by Jerusalem, for it is the city of the Great King. And do not swear by your head, for you cannot make even one hair white or black.** All you need to say is simply "Yes" or "No"; anything beyond this comes from the evil one [or from evil]. (Matthew 5:33–37 NIV, bold added)

Consider that your steps toward sinning and condemnation are evil thoughts, then evil words, then evil actions. Some evil actions may be in retaliation to what you said in anger. When you speak violently against anyone else, aren't you making them your enemy and not your beloved neighbor? James 3:12–13 further explains that judging someone else without mercy is wrong. Mercy is to consider the other person's side of the story and being able to forgive them.

Speak and act as those who are going to be judged by the law that gives freedom, because judgment without mercy will be shown to anyone who has not been merciful. **Mercy triumphs over judgment** [condemnation]. (James 3:12 NIV, bold added)

James 4:1–3 (NIV, bold added) further explains that quarreling with others can come from your wanting what you don't have, being envious, or being jealous:

What causes fights and quarrels among you? Don't they come from your desires that battle within you? You desire but do not have, so you kill. **You covet but you cannot get what you want, so you quarrel and fight.** You do not have because you do not ask God. When you ask, you do not receive, because you ask with wrong motives, that you may spend what you get on your pleasures.

God has many similar references where controlling what you say is vitally important. Some examples of this are in Matthew 12:34–37, Matthew 15:9–20, and Job 27:3:

You brood of vipers, how can you who are evil say anything good? **For the mouth speaks what the heart is full of.** A good man brings good things out of the good stored up in him, and an evil man brings evil things out of the evil stored up in him. But I tell you that everyone will have to give account on the day of judgment for every empty word they have spoken. **For by your words you will be acquitted, and by your words you will be condemned.** (Matthew 12:34–37 NIV, bold added)

"They worship Me in vain; their teachings are merely human rules." Jesus called the crowd to Him and said,

"Listen and understand. What goes into someone's mouth does not defile them, but **what comes out of their mouth, that is what defiles them.**" Then the disciples came to Him and asked, "Do you know that the Pharisees were offended when they heard this?" He replied, "Every plant that My heavenly Father has not planted will be pulled up by the roots. Leave them; they are blind guides. If the blind lead the blind, both will fall into a pit." Peter said, "Explain the parable to us." "Are you still so dull?" Jesus asked them. "Don't you see that whatever enters the mouth goes into the stomach and then out of the body? **But the things that come out of a person's mouth come from the heart, and these defile them. For out of the heart come evil thoughts—murder, adultery, sexual immorality, theft, false testimony, slander. These are what defile a person; but eating with unwashed hands does not defile them.**" (Matthew 15:9–20 NIV, bold added)

As long as I have life within me, the breath of God in my nostrils, **my lips will not say anything wicked, and my tongue will not utter lies.** (Job 27:3–4 NIV, bold added)

In conclusion, the Bible fully recognizes that it's difficult to control what you say, how you speak to your family and neighbors, and what you say about your neighbors. That is why you need to practice controlling your anger and your disrespectful thoughts about others, in order to stay on the narrow path that takes you to heaven.

CHAPTER 10

WHAT WORKS AND DEEDS ARE IMPORTANT?

There are two kinds of work, like there are two kinds of wisdom: heavenly and earthly. Earthly work includes making things, such as houses, buildings, cities, and empires. Earthly work includes the labor done to earn money, to make a living. All these things and works will eventually pass away. Even the great pyramids of Egypt, which have stood for thousands of years, will eventually erode away. And everyone's body eventually fails and decays away, along with their lifetime of earthly accomplishments.

Heavenly works, only from a human perspective, may appear to be temporary. However, all your works and actions are eternally important to an all-knowing God, Who never forgets anything. God, Who has always been, is now, and ever shall be, is the One Who remembers and judges all your works and actions while you're alive. He is the only One Who can weigh your works as righteous or heavenly and then judge if you should receive His eternal blessings. James expounds on the idea of earthly versus heavenly works in the following passages:

Believers in humble circumstances ought to take pride in their high position. But the rich should take pride in their humiliation—since they will pass away like a wild flower. For the sun rises with scorching heat and withers the plant; its blossom falls and its beauty is destroyed. **In the same way, the rich will fade away even while they go about their business. Blessed is the one who perseveres under trial because, having stood the test, that person will receive the crown of life that the Lord has promised to those who love him**. (James 1:9–12 NIV, bold added)

Who is wise and understanding among you? **Let them show it by their good life, by deeds done in the humility that comes from wisdom**. But if you harbor bitter envy and selfish ambition in your hearts, do not boast about it or deny the truth. Such "wisdom" does not come down from heaven but is earthly, unspiritual, demonic. For where you have envy and selfish ambition, there you find disorder and every evil practice. But the wisdom that comes from heaven is first of all pure; then peace-loving, considerate, submissive, full of mercy and good fruit, impartial and sincere. **Peacemakers who sow in peace reap a harvest of righteousness**. (James 3:13–18 NIV, bold added)

What causes fights and quarrels among you? Don't they come from your desires that battle within you? You desire but do not have, so you kill. You covet but you cannot get what you want, so you quarrel and fight. You do not have because you do not ask God. When you ask, you do not receive, because you ask with wrong motives, that you may spend what you get on your pleasures. **You adulterous people, don't you know that friendship with the world means enmity against God? Therefore, anyone who chooses to be a friend of the world becomes an enemy**

of God. Or do you think scripture says without reason that he jealously longs for the spirit he has caused to dwell in us? But he gives us more grace. That is why scripture says: "God opposes the proud but shows favor to the humble." **Submit yourselves, then, to God. Resist the devil, and he will flee from you. Come near to God and he will come near to you.** (James 4:1–8 NIV, bold added)

Now listen, you who say, "Today or tomorrow we will go to this or that city, spend a year there, carry on business and make money." Why, you do not even know what will happen tomorrow. **What is your life? You are a mist that appears for a little while and then vanishes. Instead, you ought to say, "If it is the Lord's will, we will live and do this or that."** As it is, you boast in your arrogant schemes. All such boasting is evil. If anyone, then, knows the good they ought to do and doesn't do it, it is sin for them. (James 4:13–17 NIV, bold added)

Now listen, you rich people, weep and wail because of the misery that is coming on you. Your wealth has rotted, and moths have eaten your clothes. Your gold and silver are corroded. Their corrosion will testify against you and eat your flesh like fire. You have hoarded wealth in the last days. Look! The wages you failed to pay the workers who mowed your fields are crying out against you. The cries of the harvesters have reached the ears of the Lord Almighty. **You have lived on earth in luxury and self-indulgence. You have fattened yourselves in the day of slaughter.** You have condemned and murdered the innocent one, who was not opposing you. (James 5:1–6 NIV, bold added)

The works of a righteous person are also discussed in Job 23:10–12, 29:7–17, 31:1 and 31:15-33.

But He knows the way that I take; when He has tested me, I will come forth as gold. My feet have closely followed His steps; I have kept to His way without turning aside. **I have not departed from the commands of His lips; I have treasured the words of His mouth more than my daily bread.** (Job 23:10–12 NIV, bold added)

When I went to the gate of the city and took my seat in the public square, the young men saw me and stepped aside and the old men rose to their feet; the chief men refrained from speaking and covered their mouths with their hands; the voices of the nobles were hushed, and their tongues stuck to the roof of their mouths. Whoever heard me spoke well of me, and those who saw me commended me, because **I rescued the poor who cried for help, and the fatherless who had none to assist them. The one who was dying blessed me; I made the widow's heart sing. I put on righteousness as my clothing; justice was my robe and my turban. I was eyes to the blind and feet to the lame. I was a father to the needy; I took up the case of the stranger. I broke the fangs of the wicked and snatched the victims from their teeth.** (Job 29:7–17 NIV, bold added)

Doing good works is important, but it's also important not to do things that are sinful. Job 31:1 and 15–33 also list things that a righteous man must not do:

- look lustfully at a young woman
- show favoritism
- deny the needs of the poor or widows
- keep food to yourself, not sharing it with the fatherless
- allow anyone to perish for lack of clothing, or keep the needy without garments

- raise a hand against the fatherless
- put trust in gold or saying pure gold is your security
- rejoice over great wealth
- worship the sun in its radiance or the moon moving in its splendor
- rejoice at an enemy's misfortune or gloat over the trouble that came to that person
- allow your mouth to sin by invoking a curse against another's life
- allow a stranger to spend the night in the street
- conceal your sin by hiding your guilt in your heart

Furthermore, in Leviticus 19:1–18, God tells Moses several things that He wants us to do to become more righteous:

- be holy because the LORD your God is holy
- respect your mother and father
- observe the Sabbath
- do not turn to idols or make metal gods
- sacrifice a fellowship offering to the Lord in an acceptable
- do not reap to the very edges of your field or gather the gleanings of your harvest
- leave some of the harvest for the poor and the foreigner
- do not steal
- do not lie
- do not deceive one another
- do not swear falsely by the Lord's name
- do not defraud or rob your neighbor
- do not hold back the wages of a hired worker overnight
- do not curse the deaf or put a stumbling block in front of the blind, but fear God
- do not pervert justice
- do not show partiality to the poor or favoritism to the great
- judge your neighbor fairly

- do not spread slander
- do not endanger your neighbor's life
- do not hate a person in your heart
- rebuke your neighbor frankly so you not share in their guilt
- do not seek revenge or bear a grudge against anyone
- love your neighbor as yourself

Everything that you think, say, and do is known by God. You need to plan and train all your thoughts, words, and actions to be pleasing to God. His perfect accounting of your entire life, which includes how you lived it, your love for the Lord, your love for your neighbors, and your disdain of sinful ways and evil, will yield your ultimate fate, which rests solely on His perfect judgment.

CHAPTER 11

DO YOU JUDGE OTHERS?

Judging others; what does that mean? It is so easy to say your next-door neighbor has a shabby lawn, an in-law has the wrong political stance, or someone drinks too much. These are things that you can observe and support with facts to form an opinion. But is this judging another person or, more importantly, their soul? Judging another person, within the context of the Bible, is making a decision as to whether a person is bound for heaven or hell. You really can't make that kind of judgment, because you are not all-knowing. James 2:12–13, 4:11–12, and 5:9, and Matthew 7:1–6 discuss judging other people:

> Speak and act as those who are going to be judged by the law that gives freedom, because judgment without mercy will be shown to anyone who has not been merciful. **Mercy triumphs over judgment.** (James 2:12–13 NIV, bold added)

> **Brothers and sisters, do not slander one another.** Anyone who speaks against a brother or sister or judges them speaks

against the law and judges it. When you judge the law, you are not keeping it, but sitting in judgment on it. There is only one Lawgiver and Judge, the one Who is able to save and destroy. But you—who are you to judge your neighbor? (James 4:11–12 NIV, bold added)

Don't grumble against one another, brothers and sisters, or you will be judged. The Judge is standing at the door! (James 5:9 NIV, bold added)

Do not judge, or you too will be judged. For in the same way you judge others, you will be judged, and with the measure you use, it will be measured to you. Why do you look at the speck of sawdust in your brother's eye and pay no attention to the plank in your own eye? How can you say to your brother, "Let me take the speck out of your eye," when all the time there is a plank in your own eye? You hypocrite, first take the plank out of your own eye, and then you will see clearly to remove the speck from your brother's eye. Do not give dogs what is sacred; do not throw your pearls to pigs. If you do, they may trample them under their feet, and turn and tear you to pieces. (Matthew 7:1–6 NIV, bold added)

So what should you do if you are called for jury duty or are a judge in a court of law? In every case that goes to trial, give careful consideration to the evidence that is presented. You are judging the evidence as factual or false to determine if a person or company has broken a secular law. Many human-made rules and laws are similar to God's laws, such as not stealing, not murdering, and not giving false testimony. There is a need to judge the facts in a case and decide if a person is guilty of breaking the government's laws, rules, and regulations or not. But you are not judging that person's soul and saying whether or not that person is evil and should be condemned to hell.

This brings up an interesting question about a court sentencing a person to death, after being found guilty of a heinous crime. The laws of a country or a state may allow for the death penalty, which is essentially government-sponsored murder. God's law simply states that you shall not murder. Are those who support capital murder guilty of breaking God's sixth commandment?

Can you recognize a sin, and should you point out that sin to the person who commits it? Earlier, in Matthew 7:1–6, it says to remove the sin (speck of sawdust) from your brother, after you have fully examined yourself and removed any sins from your own life. James 5:19–20 and 3:1–2 say more about telling or teaching others about their sins.

> My brothers and sisters, if one of you should wander from the truth and someone should bring that person back, remember this: **Whoever turns a sinner from the error of their way will save them from death and cover over a multitude of** [their own] **sins.** (James 5:19–20 NIV, bold added)

> **Not many of you should become teachers, my fellow believers, because you know that we who teach will be judged more strictly.** We all stumble in many ways. Anyone who is never at fault in what they say is perfect, able to keep their whole body in check. (James 3:1–2 NIV, bold added)

Before you try to help someone confront a sinful way, tell that person that you are imperfect and a sinner too. James 5:16 (NIV) reinforces this idea:

> Therefore confess your sins to each other and pray for each other so that you may be healed. The prayer of a righteous person is powerful and effective.

The wisdom given in James on how to correct the sins of others doesn't say "Love the sinner; hate the sin." And this specific phrase is not in the Bible, but the same intent is found in Jude 1:22–23 (NIV):

> Be merciful to those who doubt [nonbelievers]; save others by snatching them from the fire; to others show mercy, mixed with fear—hating even the clothing stained by corrupted flesh.

Leading by your example can be a very effective means to teach others the errors of their ways: "For it is God's will that by doing good you should silence the ignorant talk of foolish people." (1 Peter 1:15 NIV)

Another way to allow your judgment of others to ruin your life is to compare yourself to others. Could you say, my neighbor has committed adultery dozens of times, so I'm not so bad for just doing it once? Isn't rationalizing your sins making you the judge of God's commandments, and then, who do you think you are?

CHAPTER 12

ARE YOU A FRIEND OF THE WORLD?

If you don't believe in God, heaven, or hell, you may only be concerned about yourself during your short life here on earth. If that were the case, couldn't you do anything you want, with no moral limitations, as long as you don't get caught? Even atheists can have a sense of morality and the capability to love and the desire to be loved by others, which may be the prime reason most people behave in a civilized manner. Thus, people are not 100 percent self-centered all the time. This is how God makes people different from wild animals; it's what gives us the ability to love. It can't be explained as a biological trait that evolved over the centuries. If that were true, all the other animals, who have been here just as long as we have, would have also evolved with the same characteristics as humans. The simple answer is that we are made in the image of God, Who is a merciful and loving God.

Love, morality, faith, desire, and other emotions are not physical things that can be humanly measured or quantified. They are related to thoughts and ideas that only each individual can experience and express. How these emotions relate to the physical world is a subject discussed in James 1:27 and 4:1–8, where James clarifies what friendship with the world is:

> **Religion that God our Father accepts as pure and faultless is this: to look after orphans and widows in their distress and to keep oneself from being polluted by the world.** (James 1:27 NIV, bold added)

> What causes fights and quarrels among you? **Don't they come from your desires that battle within you? You desire but do not have, so you kill. You covet but you cannot get what you want, so you quarrel and fight.** You do not have because you do not ask God. When you ask, you do not receive, **because you ask with wrong motives, that you may spend what you get on your pleasures.** You adulterous people, **don't you know that friendship with the world means enmity against God? Therefore, anyone who chooses to be a friend of the world becomes an enemy of God.** Or do you think scripture says without reason that he jealously longs for the spirit he has caused to dwell in us? But he gives us more grace. **That is why scripture says: "God opposes the proud but shows favor to the humble."** Submit yourselves, then, to God. Resist the devil, and he will flee from you. **Come near to God and he will come near to you. Wash your hands, you sinners, and purify your hearts, you double-minded.** (James 4:1–8 NIV, bold added)

The question is, are you a friend of the world? Are you focused on gaining worldly possessions, power, or status? Or are you more concerned about leading a Godly life on this earth and for all eternity? Ask yourself, "Am I selfish, or do I care about others just as much as I care about myself?"

CHAPTER 13

WILL YOU ACT TODAY, OR ONLY LISTEN TO WHAT YOU MUST DO?

Considering there is so little time in our lives to start becoming righteous, you should start as soon as possible. James explains this concept further:

> Now listen, you who say, "Today or tomorrow we will go to this or that city, spend a year there, carry on business and make money." **Why, you do not even know what will happen tomorrow.** What is your life? You are a mist that appears for a little while and then vanishes. Instead, you ought to say, "If it is the Lord's will, we will live and do this or that." As it is, you boast in your arrogant schemes. All such boasting is evil. **If anyone, then, knows the good they ought to do and doesn't do it, it is sin for them.** (James 4:13–17 NIV, bold added)

Why is it evil to boast about your plans for the future? Only God is all knowing, and only He knows which day will be your final one on earth. So if you think you are certain (arrogantly boastful) of things you will accomplish in the future, who do you think you are? You should hope and pray for a long life, so that you can grow wiser and gain more knowledge and understanding of God's will for every day of your life on this planet and then later in heaven.

James 4:17 has a stern warning about inaction. Every day, in every situation, you have a choice: to act or do nothing. If you encounter a situation where an unselfish act of kindness is appropriate, you should take the opportunity to do something. Through God-inspired wisdom, you will learn about the many good deeds that you need to accomplish each and every day of your life. Years ago, a few monks and nuns thought that the way to have a sinless life was to lock themselves inside a monastery, away from all earthly temptations. They led lives of poverty, without extravagances, and some in total silence. How many good works could they have done if they were out in society? Perhaps they knew they could do the most good in a monastery in prayer for the people outside their cell walls. Only God knows the answers to their righteousness, while in a monastery.

The book of James has more insights on how both your words and actions are both important; and addresses how religion should be practiced in James 1:19–27.

> My dear brothers and sisters, take note of this: Everyone should be quick to listen, slow to speak and slow to become angry, because human anger does not produce the righteousness that God desires. **Therefore, get rid of all moral filth and the evil that is so prevalent and humbly accept the word planted in you, which can save you. Do not merely listen to the word, and so deceive yourselves. Do what it says.** Anyone who listens to the word but does not do what it says is like someone who looks at his face in a mirror and, after looking at himself, goes away and immediately forgets what he looks like. But whoever looks intently into the perfect law that gives freedom, and

continues in it—**not forgetting what they have heard, but doing it**—they will be blessed in what they do. **Those who consider themselves religious and yet do not keep a tight rein on their tongues deceive themselves, and their religion is worthless. Religion that God our Father accepts as pure and faultless is this: to look after orphans and widows in their distress and to keep oneself from being polluted by the world.** (James 1:19–27 NIV, bold added)

CHAPTER 14

WHAT ELSE SHOULD YOU PRAY FOR?

You should pray for heavenly wisdom, but what else should you pray for? James 5:13–18 (NIV, bold added) helps you identify what else to pray for:

> **Is anyone among you in trouble? Let them pray.** Is anyone happy? Let them sing songs of praise. Is anyone among you sick? Let them call the elders of the church to **pray over them** and anoint them with oil in the name of the Lord. And **the prayer offered in faith will make the sick person well**; the Lord will raise them up. If they have sinned, they will be forgiven. Therefore **confess your sins to each other and pray for each other so that you may be healed. The prayer of a righteous person is powerful and effective.** Elijah was a human being, even as we are. **He prayed earnestly** that it would not rain, and it did not rain on the land for three and a half years. Again he prayed, and the heavens gave rain, and the earth produced its crops.

Be patient after asking your prayers; it may take years for God to answer them. And never be disappointed and disrespectful of God if His answer to your prayer is no. After all, He knows the perfect answers to all your prayers.

Please note that James says to "anoint them [the sick] with oil." For the Hebrews, olive oil was used for cooking, treating wounds, and anointing new kings and religious leaders. When the book of James is being written, olive oil and herbs are the medicines available at that time. This is saying that use of medicine is a sound practice for healing the sick, along with prayers. Some people think that the use of medicine or blood transfusions is not God's way of healing. They believe that with enough faith alone, God will heal anyone. Who do you think gave humans the knowledge to invent and use the medicines and medical techniques to heal the sick and injured? Using modern medicine seems just as logical as anointing with oil, back when medical practices were much less developed.

Pray for heavenly wisdom, the healing of the sick, the elimination of disobedience to God and His laws, and the patience and persistence to see and understand all of God's answers to your prayers, which may be answered with yes, no, or later. Don't pray for your worldly desires. James 4:3 (NIV) says, "When you ask, you do not receive, because you ask with wrong motives, that you may spend what you get on your pleasures."

CHAPTER 15

WHY IS THE BOOK OF JAMES THE PRECIOUS PEARL?

There are several reasons to consider the book of James to be a precious pearl, one that you should give up everything else to possess. The prime reason is that it logically and clearly lays out what we must do to receive salvation. It references the Ten Commandments, which must be followed to become righteous. It tells us to love and help our neighbors and not to judge or condemn them. It tells us to love, trust, obey, and praise God in all circumstances, just like Job does. It also tells us to control what we say and how we speak to each other. The book of James is a relatively short and clear guide to what we must do and not do to earn salvation, through both our faith and our works.

The book of James doesn't come up with a new doctrine about salvation that is different from the Old Testament. If this book professed a new and different way to reach salvation, it would indicate that God had changed over time. Can a god that changes over time be trusted? James accurately references the Old Testament several times, which is not what Stephen did in Acts. (See section 16.2.)

Consistency with the Old Testament is essential to ensuring your path to salvation does not take off in a new direction, which may not be the original path defined by a perfect and unchanging God.

James is internally consistent in his message throughout his book, unlike others, who seem to say two contradictory things. (See this book's first chapter and section 16.3.) The book of James is written in a clear and understandable manner. It presents a well-planned approach to improve ourselves and walk on the narrow path we must follow on our way to salvation. The book of James also addresses the important points needed for your religious life.

CHAPTER 16

ARE THERE CONTRADICTORY PASSAGES IN THE BIBLE?

Questioning the accuracy of the words in the Bible may seem like blasphemy, if you think that every word in the Holy Bible is the perfect Word of God. But if the words in one part of the Bible directly contradict the words in another part of the Bible, there is no judgment of God's perfect words, because a perfect God cannot contradict Himself. Finding directly contradictory theological concepts can only conclude that one or both of the concepts are in error. Hopefully, one of the concepts is true, while the other contradictory concept is false. Some Bible scholars may be afraid that if there is even one false concept is in the Bible, that the entire Bible must be dismissed as unreliable. That seems to be a nonsensical notion, if you keep in mind that all the words in the Bible are written by humans.

So how do you separate the weeds from the wheat in the Bible? That is difficult question to answer, but it can be found by using God-given logic and heavenly wisdom. Logic says that when theological concepts are consistent from the beginning of the document to the end, the likelihood is greater that they are correct. Again, a perfect God cannot and will not change the rules for us in the middle of the stream. Also, God will give us heavenly wisdom when we sincerely ask for it. I hope He gives it to you, just as I trust He gave it to me, over the many years I've been seeking God's absolute truth in the Bible.

The following examples demonstrate how one part of the Bible contradicts another part of the Bible. These examples will hopefully help you to start thinking objectively, logically, and wisely to begin your search for the whole truth, which definitely is in the Bible.

16.1. How Many Roads Lead to Damascus?

There are three versions of Saul's story of his conversion to become a Christian, while traveling on the road to Damascus. As I said in Chapter 1, when police detectives question a suspect, they have the suspect repeat his story or alibi several times, looking for inconsistencies in the various versions of their stories. Significant inconsistencies in the various story versions raise questions about the suspect's honesty. There are contradictions between the three stories of Saul's miraculous encounter with the Lord and his conversion to become a follower of Christ. Analysis of Saul's three versions of his trip to Damascus, raise questions about his telling his story consistently. The following are the three versions of Saul's miraculous meeting with the Lord:

Version 1

> As he neared Damascus on his journey, suddenly a light from heaven flashed around him. He fell to the ground and heard a voice say to him, "Saul, Saul, why do you persecute

Me?" "Who are you, Lord?" Saul asked. "I am Jesus, whom you are persecuting," He replied. "Now get up and go into the city, and you will be told what you must do." The men traveling with Saul stood there speechless; they heard the sound but did not see anyone. Saul got up from the ground, but when he opened his eyes he could see nothing. So they led him by the hand into Damascus. For three days he was blind, and did not eat or drink anything. In Damascus there was a disciple named Ananias. The Lord called to him in a vision, "Ananias!" "Yes, Lord," he answered. The Lord told him, "Go to the house of Judas on Straight Street and ask for a man from Tarsus named Saul, for he is praying. In a vision he has seen a man named Ananias come and place his hands on him to restore his sight." "Lord," Ananias answered, "I have heard many reports about this man and all the harm he has done to your holy people in Jerusalem. And he has come here with authority from the chief priests to arrest all who call on Your name." But the Lord said to Ananias, "Go! This man is My chosen instrument to proclaim My name to the Gentiles and their kings and to the people of Israel. I will show him how much he must suffer for My name." Then Ananias went to the house and entered it. Placing his hands on Saul, he said, "Brother Saul, the Lord—Jesus, Who appeared to you on the road as you were coming here—has sent me so that you may see again and be filled with the Holy Spirit." Immediately, something like scales fell from Saul's eyes, and he could see again. He got up and was baptized, and after taking some food, he regained his strength. Saul spent several days with the disciples in Damascus. (Acts 9:3–18 NIV)

Version 2

About noon as I came near Damascus, suddenly a bright light from heaven flashed around me. I fell to the ground and heard a voice say to me, "Saul! Saul! Why do you persecute me?" "Who are you, Lord?" I asked. "I am Jesus of Nazareth, Whom you are persecuting," He replied. My companions saw the light, but they did not understand the voice of Him Who was speaking to me. "What shall I do, Lord?" I asked. "Get up," the Lord said, "and go into Damascus. There you will be told all that you have been assigned to do." My companions led me by the hand into Damascus, because the brilliance of the light had blinded me. A man named Ananias came to see me. He was a devout observer of the law and highly respected by all the Jews living there. He stood beside me and said, "Brother Saul, receive your sight!" And at that very moment I was able to see him. Then he said: "The God of our ancestors has chosen you to know his will and to see the Righteous One and to hear words from his mouth. You will be his witness to all people of what you have seen and heard. And now what are you waiting for? Get up, be baptized and wash your sins away, calling on His name." (Acts 22:6–16 NIV)

Version 3

About noon, King Agrippa, as I was on the road, I saw a light from heaven, brighter than the sun, blazing around me and my companions. We all fell to the ground, and I heard a voice saying to me in Aramaic, "Saul, Saul, why do you persecute me? It is hard for you to kick against the goads." Then I asked, "who are you, Lord?" "I am Jesus, Whom you are persecuting," the Lord replied. "Now get up and stand on your feet. I have appeared to you to appoint you as a servant and as a witness of what you have seen and will see of Me. I will rescue you from your own people and from the Gentiles. I am sending you to them to open their eyes and turn them from darkness to light, and from the power of Satan to God, so that they may receive forgiveness of sins and a place among those who are sanctified by faith in me." So then, King Agrippa, I was not disobedient to the vision from heaven. First to those in Damascus, then to those in Jerusalem and in all Judea, and then to the Gentiles, I preached that they should repent and turn to God and demonstrate their repentance by their deeds. (Acts 26:13–20 NIV)

The differences in these three recitations of Saul's trip to Damascus are individually contrasted in the following:

Version 1: He fell to the ground and heard a voice say to him, "Saul, Saul, why do you persecute me?" (Acts 9:4 NIV)

Version 2: I fell to the ground and heard a voice say to me, "Saul! Saul! Why do you persecute me?" (Acts 22:7 NIV)

Version 3: We all fell to the ground, and I heard a voice saying to me in Aramaic, "Saul, Saul, why do you persecute me? It is hard for you to kick against the goads." (Acts 26:14 NIV)

and:

Version 1: "Who are you, Lord?" Saul asked. "I am Jesus, Whom you are persecuting," He replied. "Now get up and go into the city, and you will be told what you must do." (Acts 9:5 NIV)

Version 2: "Who are you, Lord?" I asked. "I am Jesus of Nazareth, Whom you are persecuting," He replied. ... "What shall I do, Lord?" I asked. "Get up," the Lord said, "and go into Damascus. There you will be told all that you have been assigned to do." (Acts 22:8 NIV)

Version 3: Then I asked, "Who are you, Lord?" "I am Jesus, whom you are persecuting," the Lord replied. "Now get up and stand on your feet. I have appeared to you to appoint you as a servant and as a witness of what you have seen and will see of Me. I will rescue you from your own people and from the Gentiles. I am sending you to them to open their eyes and turn them from darkness to light, and from the power of Satan to God, so that they may receive forgiveness of sins and a place among those who are sanctified by faith in Me." (Acts 26:15–18 NIV)

If God were to speak directly to you, wouldn't you take each and every word He says to be perfect and not alter any of His words, for any reason at all? Why are Saul's quotes of what Jesus says to him so different? In Versions 1 and 2, Jesus tells Saul that he will be told what to do when he gets to Damascus. In Version 3, the Lord tells Saul what he must do before he reaches the city of Damascus.

Version 1: He fell to the ground.... The men traveling with Saul stood there speechless. (Acts 9:4 NIV)

Version 2: I fell to the ground. (Acts 22:7 NIV)

Version 3: We all fell to the ground. (Acts 26:14 NIV)

Which is it? Did they all fall to the ground, or did only Saul fall to the ground? It seems like after Saul had told the story at least twice, he would honestly remember it the same way.

Version 1: As he neared Damascus on his journey, suddenly a light from heaven flashed around him.... The men traveling with Saul stood there speechless; they heard the sound but did not see anyone. (Acts 9:3 NIV)

Version 2: About noon as I came near Damascus, suddenly a bright light from heaven flashed around me.... My companions saw the light. (Acts 22:6 NIV)

Version 3: I was on the road, I saw a light from heaven, brighter than the sun, blazing around me and my companions. (Acts 26:13 NIV)

Was the flashing-bright light only seen by Saul, or by all of his companions? If the blazing light was around both Saul and his companions, why weren't they blinded as well?

Version 1: Then Ananias went to the house and entered it. Placing his hands on Saul, he said, "Brother Saul, the Lord—Jesus, Who appeared to you on the road as you were coming here—has sent me so that you may see again and be filled with the Holy Spirit." Immediately, something like scales fell from Saul's eyes, and he could see again. He got up and was baptized. (Acts 9:17 NIV)

Version 2: My companions saw the light, but they did not understand the voice of Him Who was speaking to me. "What shall I do, Lord?" I asked. "Get up," the Lord said, "and go into Damascus. There you will be told all that you have been assigned to do." My companions led me by the hand into Damascus, because the brilliance of the light had blinded me.... He [Ananias] stood beside me and said, "Brother Saul, receive your sight!" And at that very moment I was able to see him. (Acts 22:9–13 NIV)

> **Version 3**: Acts 26 makes no mention of Saul losing or regaining his sight.

So was Saul blinded and forgot to tell King Agrippa about the miracle of his sight being healed? Seems like this is an important fact to make Saul's story more fantastic and miraculous. And was Saul cured by the "laying on of hands" or just by Ananias speaking five words?

> **Version 1**: For three days he was blind, and did not eat or drink anything. In Damascus there was a disciple named Ananias.... "Lord," Ananias answered, "I have heard many reports about this man and all the harm he has done to Your holy people in Jerusalem. And he has come here with authority from the chief priests to arrest all who call on Your name." (Acts 9:9–14 NIV)

> **Version 2:** A man named Ananias came to see me. He was a devout observer of the law and highly respected by all the Jews living there. (Acts 22:12 NIV)

> **Version 3**: Acts 26 makes no mention of Ananias.

Was Ananias a disciple of Christ and feared Saul, or was he a respected Jew who had no fear of Saul? This is an important distinction. Saul and other observers of the Jewish laws were the ones who wanted Christ crucified and then went about persecuting the new disciples of Christ. If Ananias was a disciple of Christ, he would not be respected by all the Jews, but he would be hated by the Jews for believing that Jesus Christ is the Lord.

Again, when looking for the truth, inconsistencies in the same story, repeated several times, raise questions about the validity of the storyteller.

16.2. Who Was the First Christian Martyr?

Acts 6 and 7, tells the story of Stephen, who was chosen among seven men, "known to be full of the Spirit and wisdom," (Acts 6:3 NIV) to assist the twelve apostles of Christ. Here Stephen is described as, "a man full of faith and of the Holy Spirit (Acts 6:5 NIV), as "a man full of God's grace and power," and who "performed great wonders and signs among the people." (Acts 6:8 NIV) When Jews began to argue with Stephen; "they could not stand up against the wisdom the Spirit gave him as he spoke." (Acts 6:10 NIV)

The Jews secretly persuade some to say, "We have heard Stephen speak **blasphemous words against Moses and against God**." (Acts 6:11 NIV, bold added) The Jews then incite the people, elders and teachers of the law against Stephen, seize him and bring him to trial in the Sanhedrin. They also produce false witnesses to testify against Stephen. At the trial, "All who were sitting in the Sanhedrin looked intently at Stephen, and they saw that his face was like the face of an angel." (Acts 6:15 NIV)

For the Israelites, stoning to death was a requirement for blasphemy. (see Leviticus 24:10–23) Webster's New World College Dictionary defines blasphemy as "profane or contemptuous speech, writing, or action concerning God or anything held as divine; any remark or action held to be irreverent or disrespectful; any remark deliberately mocking or contemptuous of God." (www.thoughtco.com/what-is-blasphemy-700714) The act of blasphemy is so serious that in Matthew 12:31 (NIV) it says, "And so I tell you, every kind of sin and slander can be forgiven, but blasphemy against the Spirit will not be forgiven." Jesus, the Son of God, is accused of blasphemy and the Jewish high priest condemned Him as worthy of death. (See Matthew 26:64–68, Mark 14:62–64 and John 10:31–33.) If you have ever wondered if Jesus is God, you need to read Lee Strobel's book, *The Case for Christ*. This excellent book gives the evidence, beyond any doubt, to fully support the claim that Jesus made, which led to His crucifixion.

At Stephen's trial, "the high priest asked Stephen, 'Are these charges (of blasphemy) true?'" (Acts 7:1 NIV) This leads into Stephen's testimony, where he attempts to recite various parts of the Old Testament. The following are sections of essentially the trial transcript of Stephen's testimony, given in Acts 7. After some of Stephen's inconsistent recitation of scripture, a comment is made about what actually appears in the Old Testament.

> Then the high priest asked Stephen, "Are these charges true?" To this he replied: "Brothers and fathers, listen to me! The God of glory appeared to our father Abraham while he was still in Mesopotamia, **before he lived in Harran**. (Acts 7:1–2 NIV, bold added)

Comment: The Lord spoke to Abram (Abraham) when he was living in Harran, not before then; see Genesis 11:31–32 and 12:1–4.

> "Leave your country and your people," God said, "and go to the land I will show you." So he [Abraham] left the land of the Chaldeans and settled in Harran. **After the death of his father God sent him to this land** where you are now living. [Israel was called the land of Canaan.] (Acts 7:3–4 NIV, bold added)

Comment: Abram left Harran and settled in Canaan, per Genesis 12:1-5. He took his wife Sarai, his nephew Lot, all the possessions they had accumulated, and the people they had acquired in Harran, and they set out for the land of Canaan, and they arrived there. Abram's father, Terah, lived to be 205 years old and was still alive when Abram left Harran; see Genesis 11:32.

He gave him [Abraham] **no inheritance here, not even enough ground to set his foot on**. But God promised him that **he and his descendants after him would possess the land**, even though at that time Abraham had no child. (Acts 7:5 NIV, bold added)

<u>Comment</u>: It seems contradictory to say Abraham had "no inheritance" in Canaan and "that he and his descendants after him would possess the land." In Genesis 12:2, God told Abraham that He will make him into a great nation, bless him, make his name great, and that he will be a blessing. In Genesis 13:14-15 (NIV), "The LORD said to Abram after Lot had parted from him, 'Look around from where you are, to the north and south, east and west. All the land that you see I will give to you and your offspring forever.'"

God spoke to him in this way: 'For four hundred years your descendants will be strangers in a country not their own, and they will be enslaved and mistreated. But I will punish the nation they serve as slaves,' God said, 'and **afterward they will come out of that country and worship me in this place**.' (Acts 7:6-7 NIV, bold added)

<u>Comment</u>: Genesis 15:14 (NIV) actually says, "But I will punish the nation they serve as slaves, and afterward they will come out with great possessions."

On their second visit, Joseph told his brothers who he was, and Pharaoh learned about Joseph's family. After this, Joseph sent for his father Jacob and **his whole family, seventy-five in all**. (Acts 7:13 NIV, bold added)

<u>Comment</u>: Genesis 46:27 says that with Joseph's two sons, the members of Jacob's family, which went to Egypt, **were seventy in**

all. Also, in Exodus 1:5, the descendants of Jacob numbered seventy in all.

> Then Jacob went down to Egypt, where he and our ancestors died. Their **bodies were brought back to Shechem and placed in the tomb that Abraham had bought from the sons of Hamor at Shechem** for a certain sum of money. (Acts 7:15-16 NIV, bold added)

<u>Comment</u>: Stephen got it wrong as to what was bought from whom. "Then he (Jacob) gave them these instructions: 'I am about to be gathered to my people. Bury me with my fathers in the cave in the field of Ephron the Hittite, the **cave in the field of Machpelah, near Mamre in Canaan**, which **Abraham bought along with the field as a burial place from Ephron the Hittite**. There Abraham and his wife Sarah were buried, there Isaac and his wife Rebekah were buried, and there I buried Leah. The **field and the cave in it were bought from the Hittites**.'" (Genesis 49:29-32 NIV, bold added)

<u>Comment</u>: Regarding what was bought from the sons of Hamor, Genesis 33:19-20 (NIV, bold added) says "For a hundred pieces of silver, he [Jacob] **bought from the sons of Hamor, the father of Shechem**, the **plot of ground where he pitched his tent**. There he set up an altar and called it El Elohe Israel." (bold added)

> As the time drew near for God to fulfill his promise to Abraham, the number of our people in Egypt had greatly increased. Then 'a new king, to whom Joseph meant nothing, came to power in Egypt.' He dealt treacherously with our people and oppressed our ancestors by **forcing them to throw out their newborn babies so that they would die**. (Acts 7:17–19 NIV, bold added)

<u>Comment</u>: Exodus 1:15–22 (NIV, bold added) says "The king of Egypt **said to the Hebrew midwives**, whose names were Shiphrah and Puah, 'When you are helping the Hebrew women during childbirth on the delivery stool, **if you see that the baby is a boy, kill him**; but if it is a girl, let her live.' The midwives, however, feared God and did not do what the king of Egypt had told them to do; they let the boys live. Then the king of Egypt summoned the midwives asked them, 'Why have you done this? you let the boys live?' The midwives answered Pharaoh, 'Hebrew women are not like Egyptian women; they are vigorous and give birth before midwives arrive.' So God was kind to the midwives and the people increased and became even more numerous. And because the midwives feared God, he gave them families of their own. Then Pharaoh gave this order to all his people: '**Every Hebrew boy that is born you must throw into the Nile**, but let every girl live.'"

> At that time Moses was born, and he was no ordinary child. For three months he was cared for by his family. (Acts 7:20 NIV, bold added)

<u>Comment</u>: Nowhere in Exodus does it say Moses was "no ordinary child."

> When he was placed outside, Pharaoh's daughter took him and brought him up as her own son. Moses was educated in all the wisdom of the Egyptians and **was powerful in speech and action**. (Acts 7:21-22 NIV, bold added)

<u>Comment</u>: Moses being powerful in speech and action is not mentioned in Exodus, and in Exodus 4:10 (NIV), Moses himself said, "Pardon your servant, Lord. I have never been eloquent, neither in the past nor since you have spoken to your servant. **I am slow of speech and tongue**." (bold added)

When Moses was **forty years old**, he decided to visit his own people, the Israelites. He saw one of them being mistreated by an Egyptian, so he went to his defense and avenged him by killing the Egyptian. Moses **thought his own people would realize that God was using him to rescue them**, but they did not. (Acts 7:23-25 NIV, bold added)

Comment: Neither Moses's age nor what he thought is mentioned in Exodus.

The next day Moses came upon two Israelites who were fighting. He tried to reconcile them by saying, '**Men, you are brothers; why do you want to hurt each other?**' (Acts 7:26 NIV, bold added)

Comment: "The next day he went out and saw two Hebrews fighting. **He asked the one in the wrong, 'Why are you hitting your fellow Hebrew?'**" (Exodus 2:13 NIV, bold added)

But the man who was mistreating the other **pushed Moses** aside and said, "Who made you ruler and judge over us? Are you thinking of killing me as you killed the Egyptian **yesterday**?" (Acts 7:27-28 NIV, bold added)

Comment: In Exodus 2:13-14, the man did not push Moses and "yesterday" is not written.

After forty years had passed, an angel appeared to Moses in the flames of a burning bush in the desert near Mount Sinai [a.k.a. Horeb, the mountain of God]. When he saw this, he was amazed at the sight. As he went over to get a closer look, he heard the Lord say: "I am the God of your fathers, the God of Abraham, Isaac and Jacob." Moses trembled with fear and did not dare to look. (Acts 7:30–32 NIV)

<u>Comment</u>: Again, forty years is not mentioned in Exodus.

> I have indeed seen the oppression of my people in Egypt. I have heard their groaning and have come down to set them free. Now come, I will send you back to Egypt.' This is the same Moses **they** (the Hebrews) had rejected with the words, "Who made you ruler and judge?" (Acts 7:34-35 NIV, bold added)

<u>Comment</u>: "Who made you ruler and judge?" comes from Exodus 2:14 (NIV), by only one of the men who were fighting.

> But God turned away from them and gave them over to the **worship of the sun, moon and stars.** This agrees with what is written in the book of the prophets: (Acts 7:42 NIV, bold added)

<u>Comment</u>: There is no mention of the worship of the sun, moon and stars is in Exodus. Did Stephen just make this up?

> You have taken up the tabernacle of **Molek** and the star of your god **Rephan**, the idols you made to worship. Therefore I will send you into **exile' beyond Babylon.** "Our ancestors had the tabernacle of the covenant law with them in the wilderness. It had been made as God directed Moses, according to the pattern he had seen. (Acts 7:43-44 NIV, bold added)

<u>Comment</u>: The three names in bold are not mentioned in Exodus.

> When the members of the Sanhedrin heard this, they were furious and gnashed their teeth at him. But Stephen, full of the Holy Spirit, looked up to heaven and saw the glory of God, and Jesus standing at the right hand of God. "Look," he said, "I see heaven open and the Son of Man standing at the

right hand of God." At this they covered their ears and, yelling at the top of their voices, they all rushed at him, dragged him out of the city and began to stone him. Meanwhile, the witnesses laid their coats at the feet of a young man named Saul. While they were stoning him, Stephen prayed, "Lord Jesus, receive my spirit." Then he fell on his knees and cried out, "Lord, do not hold this sin against them." When he had said this, he fell asleep. (Acts 7:54-60 NIV)

After Stephen's adulteration of holy scriptures, is there any wonder why they gnashed their teeth, covered their ears, rushed him, and dragged him out of the city to be stoned? There are three possibilities regarding what is written in Acts about Stephen's testimony:

1. Stephen is accurately quoted in Acts, but he is uneducated and didn't really know the holy scriptures and is unintentionally blaspheming the Word of God. Or it could also be that Stephen was nervous at this life-threatening trial and this clouded his thoughts and testimony. If either of these is true, then this is inconsistent with Stephen's "wisdom the Spirit gave him as he spoke." (Acts 6:10 NIV)

2. Stephen is accurately quoted in Acts, but he intentionally misquotes the holy scriptures, is fully aware of his blasphemy, and knows that he will be stoned to death. This type of suicide by stoning seems unlikely.

3. Stephen is misquoted in Acts. This seems unlikely, because Stephen's word-for-word trial testimony is exactly what leads the Jews to stone him to death. What purpose would be served by inaccurately quoting Stephen? And if this is done, would this raise questions about the validity of the story about his martyrdom?

This detailed analysis of Acts 6 and 7 seems to raise several red flags about the story of Stephen. What do you think, is Stephen clearly the first Christian martyr?

16.3. What Is the Truth about the Barren Fig Tree?

There are three stories in the New Testament about a fig tree that is fruitless. These are in Matthew, Mark, and Luke.

> Early in the morning, as Jesus was on His way back to the city, He was hungry. Seeing a fig tree by the road, He went up to it but found nothing on it except leaves. Then He said to it, "May you never bear fruit again!" Immediately the tree withered. When the disciples saw this, they were amazed. "How did the fig tree wither so quickly?" they asked. Jesus replied, "Truly I tell you, if you have faith and do not doubt, not only can you do what was done to the fig tree, but also you can say to this mountain, 'Go, throw yourself into the sea,' and it will be done. If you believe, you will receive whatever you ask for in prayer." (Mathew 21:18–22 NIV)

> The next day as they were leaving Bethany, Jesus was hungry. Seeing in the distance a fig tree in leaf, He went to find out if it had any fruit. When He reached it, He found nothing but leaves, because it was not the season for figs. Then He said to the tree, "May no one ever eat fruit from you again." And His disciples heard Him say it. (Mark 11:12–14 NIV)

> In the morning, as they went along, they saw the fig tree withered from the roots. Peter remembered and said to Jesus, "Rabbi, look! The fig tree You cursed has withered!" "Have faith in God," Jesus answered. "Truly I tell you, if anyone says to this mountain, 'Go, throw yourself into the

sea,' and does not doubt in their heart but believes that what they say will happen, it will be done for them. Therefore I tell you, whatever you ask for in prayer, believe that you have received it, and it will be yours. And when you stand praying, if you hold anything against anyone, forgive them, so that your Father in heaven may forgive you your sins." (Mark 11:20–25 NIV)

He told this parable: "A man had a fig tree growing in his vineyard, and he went to look for fruit on it but did not find any. So he said to the man who took care of the vineyard, 'For three years now I've been coming to look for fruit on this fig tree and haven't found any. Cut it down! Why should it use up the soil?' 'Sir,' the man replied, 'leave it alone for one more year, and I'll dig around it and fertilize it. If it bears fruit next year, fine! If not, then cut it down.'" (Luke 13:5 NIV)

In two stories, the fruitless fig tree is killed quickly, but in the parable in Luke, the tree gets saved and has another chance to bear fruit. These two outcomes are totally opposite and thus contradictory. How can two entirely opposite messages both be true? Which is the one that you want to be true? Is it the one about God's grace and perseverance, that with the proper stimulation, you too can become fruitful and pleasing to God? I cannot guess the point of the first two stories. If they were a parable, it would relate to the false premise that God instantly punishes those who displease Him, like Job's friends telling him that he is reaping the evil that he has sown.

Again, remember that everything in the Bible is written by people, who try to say exactly what God wants them to say, but they may make some mistakes or insert words that are not from God Himself. As I said earlier, contradictions in the Bible can be distractions to God's absolute truth, but with wise discernment, His truth can absolutely be found in the Bible.

CHAPTER 17

WHY I WROTE THIS BOOK

My education is in physics, nuclear plant operations, and health physics, which is the science of radiation protection. I trained naval officers on how to safely operate a nuclear submarine and then worked for years as a health physicist, project manager, principal scientist, and radiation safety officer at a major independent research laboratory. My education and work both involve analyzing and then applying the information contained in scientific textbooks, technical operating manuals, and governmental-regulatory requirements. This experience developed my skills to read long documents in order to develop the best practices to safely operate complex systems, like a nuclear power plant, or to develop procedures for projects to safely use radiation in unique applications.

My parents raised me in the Catholic Church, and after my marriage, I joined the Methodist Church. I was not an actively practicing Christian, until my wife and I decided to send our girls to a private religious school. When they came home with homework to learn Bible passages and lessons, I decided I needed to read the Bible to see what it was all about. This was a very difficult time for me, because there seemed to be inconsistencies in the Bible. I'm not talking about minor inconsistencies, like how many people saw Jesus when he rose from the dead. I was focused on major differences in religious concepts, like are your saved by faith alone or by your works? These religious dilemmas plagued me until I got to the short book of James. After I read James, light began to fill the darkness.

After my repeated analyses of the Bible, I concluded that the book of James contains God's absolute truth, and now I want the whole world to know this too. I'm not smarter than anyone else and definitely not more schooled in the Bible, like priests and pastors; but I am convinced, on an objective and logical basis, that James is the best guide to our salvation. A more important consideration in writing this book is to hopefully turn sinners, including myself, away from damnation and to cover over the multitude of sins I have committed in my lifetime. James 5:19–20 (NIV) tells you how I hope to do this:

> My brothers and sisters, if one of you should wander from the truth and someone should bring that person back, remember this: Whoever turns a sinner from the error of their way will save them from death and cover over a multitude of sins.

But this desire to educate people in God's truth in the Bible comes with a heavy price, a price that may make my path to heaven more uncertain. James 3:1 warns, "Not many of you should become teachers, my fellow believers, because you know that we who teach will be judged more strictly." Only God knows where my soul will end up after my earthly death.

The Bible may be summarized simply with the words: do good and resist evil. The book of James adds the details needed to clarify how to lead our lives to be on the road to heaven. These are:

- Strictly obey each one of the Ten Commandments
- Treat everyone else as you want to be treated

- Control your thoughts and words out of respect for your neighbors
- Ask for Godly wisdom, and don't doubt that He will give it to you
- Pray for healing and trust God to provide His perfect answers
- Help those who need help, both physically and morally
- Learn from your failures, hardships and trials so that you become a better person
- Have patience and perseverance in all that you do
- Neither show favoritism nor judge another person
- Worldly possessions all pass away, only your righteous actions will be remembered by God
- Praise the LORD at all times, both good and bad

If you found this book of value, praise God; and please recommend it to others.

ABOUT THE AUTHOR

John Hageman's education is in physics, nuclear plant operations, and health physics, the science of radiation protection. His education and work both involve analyzing and applying information in scientific and highly technical documents. He was raised a Catholic and became Methodist. He decided to analyze the Bible and focused on major differences in religious concepts, like being saved by faith alone or by works. After reading James, light began to fill the darkness; and this is where God's absolute truth can be found. This book is his way of wanting the whole world to know this truth. The last two verses of James 5 tell how he hopes to do this. "19 My brothers and sisters, if one of you should wander from the truth and someone should bring that person back, 20 remember this: Whoever turns a sinner from the error of their way will save them from death and cover over a multitude of sins. (NIV)

Printed in the United States
By Bookmasters